Pray& Play Bible 2

Loveland, Colorado

Pray & Play Bible 2

Copyright © 2003 Group Publishing, Inc.

Visit our Website: **group.com**

Credits

Contributing Authors: Thanks to all of the authors who have contributed their wonderful ideas over the years for many of our resource books for preschoolers.
Editor: Laurie Castañeda
Creative Development Editor: Jody Brolsma
Chief Creative Officer: Joani Schultz
Copy Editor: Janis Sampson
Art Director: Kari K. Monson
Cover Art Director/Designer: Bambi Morehead
Designer: Lisa Chandler
Print Production Artist: Stephen Beer
Cover Illustrator: Garry Colby
Illustrators for Bible stories: Lynn Adams (How Peter Served Jesus), Alexander Barsky (Elijah and the Big Showdown), Paula Becker (Zacchaeus), Barbara Epstein-Eagle (David and Jonathan), Alan Flinn (The Good Samaritan), Pat Hoggan (Joseph the Favorite Son), Donna Kae Nelson (Ruth and The Easter Story), David Shaw (Daniel and His Friends), Terri Steiger (Jesus Is With Us), Dorothy Stott (Baby Moses), Kat Thacker (Creation), Mary Thelen (David and Goliath), and Jane Yamada (Jesus Is Born)
Illustrator for song pages: Ray Tollison
Illustrators for activity pages: Gioia Fiammenghi Caputo, Shelley Dieterichs, Corbin Hillam, John Jones, Emilie Kong, Bonnie Matthews, Nancy Munger, Dana Regan, and Rebecca Thornburgh
Production Manager: Peggy Naylor

Library of Congress Cataloging-in-Publication Data

Pray & play Bible 2.
        p. cm.
Summary: Contains fourteen Bible stories, plus ative prayers, playtime activities, and songs to accompany each story. ISBN 0-7644-2514-5 (a paper)
1. Bible stories, English. 2. Christian education children. [1. Bible stories. 2. Christian life.] I. T Pray and play Bible two.
II. Group Publishing.
BS551.3 .P73 2002
220.9'505--dc21
      2002010265

10 9 8 7 6   11 10 09
Printed in China

Contents

Pray & Play Bible 2
will help your kids fall in love with God's Word!

"Those who love your teachings will find true peace, and nothing will defeat them" (Psalm 119:165, New Century Version).

There's no greater joy than seeing a child fall in love with God's Word. Excited cries of "Read it again!" "This is my favorite story!" and "Let *me* tell it this time!" bring delight to the hearts of Christian parents and teachers. But helping children develop that love and understanding of the Bible can be a challenge. Often we think Bible truths are too difficult for young children to grasp, or we're not sure how to make the Bible relevant to everyday living. And sometimes family Bible study seems downright impossible with wiggly, fidgety children!

The *Pray & Play Bible 2* brings God's Word to life for little ones. These fourteen favorite Bible stories from *Group's Bible Big Books*™ and curriculum create a special Bible that children want to hear and see again and again. Through the Bible stories in this book, children will learn about God's creativity, power, and great plans for us. Most importantly, kids will discover that God loves us and sent Jesus, who died for our sins.

To help children get the most from these Bible stories, each story is written in "kid-friendly," age-appropriate language that your young child can relate to and understand. Parents, preschool teachers, and children's ministry workers across the country have watched delighted children learn Bible truths from *Group's Bible Big Books* and curriculum—and now your child can, too! The *Pray & Play Bible 2* is bursting with eye-catching, vibrant, high-quality art that entices nonreaders to explore every page in detail. But wait, there's more...

Words and pictures aren't enough to develop a passion for God's Word. Children need to use *all* of their senses to connect Bible truths to everyday life. That's why we've included three pages of activities with each story. The activities help young children and their families explore the Bible and bring it to life. Kids connect "play" with their "work" of growing up—what better way to work at learning God's Word than through play!

Since these activities have all been kid-tested, we know your child will be excited about them. Parents and teachers can be excited, too, because the activities require few supplies—most of which can be easily found around your home.

With the *Pray & Play Bible 2*, your child can learn Bible truths in many ways.

● Read a different story to your child each night before bed.

● Have your child "read" the pictures and tell you the stories.

● Use the *Pray & Play Bible 2* as a family devotional. You can focus on one story per week and do a different activity each day, or do one activity per week (you have over a year's worth of ideas!).

● Have older children use the activities to teach a story to younger siblings.

The *Pray & Play Bible 2* is designed to help children fall in love with God's Word. Psalm 119:105 affirms that "Your word is a lamp to my feet and a light for my path." May God bless you as you shine his light on the little ones in your life.

Let's Pray!

● **Creative prayers allow children a chance to communicate with God in meaningful ways.**
Children discover that prayer is more than a quiet time—it's an opportunity to talk to God, praise God, and thank God. Through unique prayer experiences, your child will learn that talking to God can be as simple as talking to a loving parent or friend.

● **Rhyming or musical prayers help children express praise and thanks in new ways.**
Use these songs, action rhymes, or finger play prayers to teach your child that prayer and praise are fun! Little ones will enjoy wearing out their wiggles with these active prayers, and you'll love seeing your child enthusiastic about praising God.

● **Simple prayers teach children that they can talk to God anytime, anywhere.**
Help your child understand that God is always nearby and that we can talk to God wherever we are. These child-friendly prayer ideas lend themselves to mealtimes, bedtimes...and to any other time!

Let's Play!

 ● **Crafts allow children to remember the Bible story through creativity.**
The crafts in this book are more than crayons, glue, and paper. They're innovative, clever, and age-appropriate activities that give kids a chance to create visual reminders of the Bible stories.

 ● **Games allow kinesthetic learners the opportunity to discover more about the Bible story through action.**
We've included simple, action-packed games that will have your child smiling and learning about God's Word at the same time.

● **Story enhancements allow children to experience the story in new ways.**
These story enhancements use finger plays, action rhymes, and drama to help your child become a part of the story and learn to tell it again and again.

 ● **Snacks allow your child to create and enjoy tasty reminders of the Bible story.**
Children love to play with their food, so we've given them a wonderful excuse to do just that! What better way for children to learn Psalm 119:103, "How sweet are your words to my taste, sweeter than honey to my mouth!"

 ● **Affirmations allow children to feel God's love in real ways.**
These unique ideas also encourage your child to express God's love to others. You'll find your child looking for positive qualities in friends, neighbors, and family members.

 ● **Service projects allow children the opportunity to act out their faith.**
What better way to help your young child develop his or her faith than by serving others. Children will understand that servanthood brings great joy!

 ● **Singing allows musical learners to remember the Bible story through simple songs.**
These action songs will keep your child singing God's Word for days! Most children are already familiar with the simple tunes, and the words will be great reminders of each Bible story.

 Be aware that some children have food allergies that can be dangerous. Know your children, and consult with parents about allergies their children may have. Also be sure to read food labels carefully, as hidden ingredients can cause allergy-related problems.

CREATION

Genesis 1:1–2:22

On the first day…

God spoke the words,
"Let there be light,"

And suddenly there was
day and night.

Darkness changed to
morning bright.

But what about the *people*?

On the second day…
God separated the sea and sky,
With water below and water up high.
And in between the air was dry.
But what about the *people*?

On the third day...
God created seas and land,
Oceans deep and
shores of sand.
Plants appeared
at God's command.
But what about the *people*?

On the fourth day...

In the sky God created lights—

Sun for days, moon and stars for nights.

Together they make such beautiful sights!

But what about the people?

On the fifth day…

God made all the fish
that swim the seas

And birds that fly up
high in the trees

To build their cozy nests
in the leaves.

But what about the *people?*

On the sixth day…

God made the animals,
big and small,

Lions fierce, giraffes so tall,

Puppies and kittens,
God made them all!

But what about
the *people*?

And finally...
God made a man from the dust
of the ground

In a beautiful
garden with
trees all around.

But a helper for Adam
could not be found

When God created *people*.

Then God took a rib
from Adam's side,

And made a woman
to be his bride.

God looked at his
people with love and
pride.

That's how God
created *people!*

In his image God
made us all.

We can listen and
answer God's call

And spread God's love to folks
big and small.

That's why God
created *people!*

All God Made

Say: **God made everything! In the beginning God created the heavens, the earth, animals, people, and everything.** God loves us so much and created such good gifts! Let's sing a song about our wonderful, loving God who created the heavens and the earth! Lead your child in singing "All God Made" to the tune of "The Farmer in the Dell."

**First God made the earth.
The heavens and the sea!
His gifts of love sent from above.
God made the earth for me.**

**And God made people, too.
Their names were Adam and Eve.
God's plan began with
just one man,
And then our God made me.**

**God made my family
To take good care of me.
His plan is good; I know we should
Be as loving as can be.**

It Was Good

Have your children create ways to act out each day as they learn the following song. For example: On day one, kids might open and close their eyes; day two, jump up high as they hold their hands up; day three, pat the ground; day four, open and close their fists like twinkling stars; day five, act like a fish or a bird; day six, shake hands; and on day seven, lie down and pretend to rest. Sing "It Was Good" to the tune of "He's Got the Whole World."

**On the first day, God made light!
And on the first day,
God made night.
On the first day, God made light.
And God saw it was good!**

**On the second day,
God made the sky
Way above our heads, oh so high!
On the second day,
God made the sky.
And God saw it was good!**

**On the third day,
God made the land
And trees and plants,
just as he'd planned!
On the third day,
God made the land.
And God saw it was good!**

**On the fourth day,
God made the sun
And the moon and stars—
he made every one!
On the fourth day,
God made the sun.
And God saw it was good!**

**On the fifth day,
God made fish and birds.
The little swimming fishies and
the flying birds.
On the fifth day,
God made fish and birds.
And God saw it was good!**

**On the sixth day, God made man
And all the animals on the land.
On the sixth day, God made man.
And God saw it was good!**

**On the seventh day,
God took a rest.
He looked around and
called it blessed.
On the seventh day,
God took a rest.
And God saw it was good!**

God Made You, God Made Me

Form a circle, and invite two or three children to stand in the center. Lead children in singing "God Made You, God Made Me" to the tune of "This Old Man." As you sing, have the children join hands and walk around the children in the center. Repeat the song until everyone has had a chance to stand in the center.

**God made you; God made me.
God made each one differently,
But we're all part of one big family.
God made each one differently.**

**God made you; God made me.
God made everyone we see,
But we're all part of one big family.
God made everyone we see.**

Let's Pray!

Thank You, God!

Teach your child this simple prayer with motions. Encourage him or her to thank God for other parts of the body as well.

**Dear God,
I thank you for my nose.
I thank you for my eyes.
I thank you for my ears that hear
And my mouth to bring you praise.
In Jesus' name, amen.**

New Ways to Pray

✔ Ask your children to look around the room or take them outside to the front of the church. Have them point out five things God created. Then lead your children in praying a thanksgiving prayer for the things and people.

✔ Invite children to remove their shoes and socks. As you and your children touch each one of your toes, take turns naming one thing that God has made. If you run out of toes to count, touch your fingers as you name even more things God has created. Then pray, thanking God for all he has created, including the toes on your feet!

✔ Plan a field trip with your family to the nearest zoo. Have your child point out the people who take care of the animals. Encourage your child to say a short simple prayer for the zookeepers, such as "Dear God, Please help the lady take good care of the monkeys."

A Wonderful World

Tell your children that they each will find a partner who will be making the same kind of animal sound as they do. Whisper into each child's ear the name of an animal, and ask the child to make the sound of that animal when you say "go." Younger children may need some help finding their partners. When kids have found their partners, have them sit down together and pray: Thank you, God, for making [let kids say the names of their animals]. Help me to take care of them for you. In Jesus' name, amen.

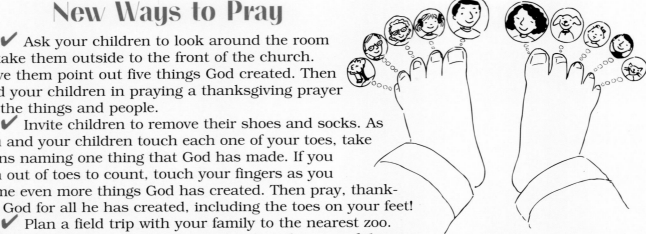

Let's Play!

Night, Light, Shining Bright

Place a large blanket over a table for kids to crawl under to experience the darkness God created. Have four to six flashlights available for children to experience the light that God created on the first day.

EXTRA IDEA! Play animal tag. Choose one child to be the "tagger." Have the tagger name an animal and then make that animal sound as he or she tries to tag other children. As children are tagged, they must join the tagger in making the animal sound. To avoid collisions, have the kids shuffle or crawl on the floor as they play. When everyone has been tagged, choose a new tagger, and let the new tagger choose another animal sound. Repeat the game as many times as kids want to play.

Flower Faces

Cut a large flower from colored construction paper for each child. Have the kids each use markers to draw a picture of themselves in the center of their flowers. (You can also take instant pictures of kids instead of having them draw their own faces.) Then attach the flowers to a bulletin board. Let children use the markers to draw stems and tear green construction paper leaves to add to the flowers. Talk about how each of us is one of God's special creations.

God Is Great!

One, two, God made you.
(Point to friend.)
Three, four, the lions roar.
(Make roaring sound.)
Five, six, God made the chicks.
(Hide arms behind back, and peck toward the floor.)
Seven, eight, God is great!
Nine, ten, let's say it again! *(Repeat as many times as you'd like.)*

Animal Buffet

Have family members wash their hands. Set out several different "animal foods" on a table. For example, you might include gummy worms for birds, carrots for rabbits, or shredded wheat "hay" for horses and cows. Let children pretend to be each animal as they sample its food. Thank God for the food he made to feed the animals.

A Caring Friend

Let your child draw pictures of their pets or pets they would like to have. Plan a class field trip to the local veterinary clinic or humane society. Let your child give his or her pictures to the doctor or person in charge as a thank you for their service to the community and for caring for God's creations.

Caring for God's World

Ask friends or neighbors if you and your child can help them walk their pets. Encourage your child to ask the owner how he or she cares for the pet. Remind your child to thank God for making pets like the one your friend or neighbor allowed you to care for.

EXTRA IDEA! The next time you visit your local park, bring along a trash bag and gloves (to protect your hands). Challenge your child to pick up ten pieces of trash to help make God's world a nicer place to play in.

JOSEPH
the Favorite Son

Genesis 37; 39:20–41:49; 42–45

Joseph was his father's favorite son. One day his father gave him a special coat.

Joseph's brothers were jealous of Joseph's coat. They threw Joseph into a deep pit.

After a while, Joseph's brothers pulled him out of the pit and sold him as a slave. Some men on camels took Joseph away to work in Egypt.

While he was in Egypt, Joseph worked for a man named Potiphar. God helped Joseph do his best work.

One day, someone told a mean lie about Joseph, and Potiphar put Joseph in jail. Even though he was in jail, Joseph knew God was with him.

The king heard that God had helped Joseph. He asked
Joseph if God could help him tell about dreams.
Joseph asked God, and God helped him tell the king
what his dreams meant.

God told Joseph that it wasn't going to rain in Egypt for a long time. That meant no food would grow. Joseph helped people save some of their food so everyone would have enough to eat.

Joseph's brothers came to Egypt to get food. God helped Joseph forgive his brothers for the mean things they'd done. Then Joseph's whole family moved to Egypt. They were happy to be together again.

Joseph Went to Sleep

Sing this song to the tune of "A Sailor Went to Sea Sea Sea."

Joseph went to sleep, sleep, sleep.
He had a dream so deep, deep, deep.
And when he woke, he shared his dream.
It made his brothers scream, scream, scream.

His brothers made him go, go, go.
Their dad would never know, know, know.
Some men bought Joseph for a slave.
He trusted God and was so brave.

Joseph's Journey

Teach your child this song to the tune of "Found a Peanut."

Got a jacket, got a jacket,
Got a jacket, just now.
Just now I got a jacket,
Got a jacket, just now.

Brothers sold me, brothers sold me,
Brothers sold me, just now.
Just now my brothers sold me,
Brothers sold me, just now.

On a journey, on a journey,
On a journey, just now.
Just now I'm on a journey,
On a journey, just now.

God will help me, God will help me,
God will help me, just now.
Just now God will help me
God will help me just now.

Forgiveness Song

Sing this song to the tune of "Mary Had a Little Lamb."

Joseph had a coat from dad, coat from dad, coat from dad.
Joseph had a coat from dad. It made his brothers mad.

They sold him to those passing by, passing by, passing by,
They sold him to those passing by and told their dad a lie.

In Egypt Joseph did so well, did so well, did so well.
In Egypt Joseph did so well. He took care of the food.

His brothers came to ask for food, ask for food, ask for food.
His brothers came to ask for food. They were in a hungry mood.

Joseph could have sent them away, sent them away, sent them away.
Joseph could have sent them away, but Joseph said, "Please stay."

God helped Joseph forgive them, forgive them, forgive them.
God helped Joseph forgive them. So they were all together again.

Let's Pray!

Help Me Serve

Remind your children that they can help others and serve God as Joseph did. Give each child a large piece of wheat cereal as a reminder about the way Joseph saved the grain in Egypt. Ask your children to wait until saying "amen" at the end of the prayer to eat their wheat rations. Lead them in repeating the following prayer. Then allow them to eat.

**Dear God,
Help me to serve you with all my
    might.
Help me to be a servant for you
In everything I say and do.
In Jesus' name, amen.**

I Forgive You

Have your kids stand in a circle. Let them take turns being "Joseph." Have Joseph wear a colorful bathrobe or long colorful shirt. Remind your children that Joseph's brothers were very mean to him, but Joseph still forgave them. Have Joseph close his eyes and spin around with one arm pointing to the circle of children. When you say "stop," have Joseph stop, open his or her eyes, and say, "I forgive you" to the child who is being pointed to. When everyone has had a chance to say, "I forgive you," lead the children in repeating the following prayer.

**Dear God,
Help us to for-
give others
as Joseph
did.
In Jesus name,
amen.**

New Ways to Pray

✔ Set out colored macaroni, and let kids sort it by colors or shapes. Remind them that God showed Joseph how to store food for the hungry people. Have the children thank God for each shape and color of food he has given them to eat.

✔ Have your children draw pictures of dreams they had. Have them hold up their pictures, and ask the children to thank God for being with them during their dreams, like the way God was with Joseph.

✔ Gather family members into a circle. Set a bowl of "Pharaoh's Dream Snack" (p. 29) in the center of the circle. Give each person a small cup. Let family members take turns going to the bowl, filling their cups, then taking them to the person sitting next to them. As each person delivers the snack, teach this prayer, "Thank you, God, that I can serve you as Joseph did." After everyone has had a turn, end the prayer by saying, "In Jesus' name, amen."

Let's Play!

Serving God

Have your children stand as you lead them in the following action rhyme.

**Joseph served God in work and
    play.** *(March in place.)*
**Joseph served God both night and
    day.** *(March in place. On "night,"
    close eyes and rest head on folded
    hands. On "day," open eyes wide, and
    open hands on both sides of face.)*
**We can serve God in work and
    play.** *(Point to self with both thumbs,
    while marching.)*
**We can serve God both night and
    day.** *(March in place, point to self,
    close eyes, and rest head on folded
    hands. Open eyes wide, and open
    hands on both sides of face.)*

Oh, Well!

 Cut butcher paper squares (about two-foot square) for each child. The squares will be the "wells." If you have a large class, create one square for every five children. Bring in a CD of the children's favorite upbeat praise music. Gather the children in small groups (about five children per group) around each well. Tell kids that Joseph was thrown into a deep pit or well. When you play the music, have the children walk around the outside of their well. When you randomly stop the music and shout, "Oh, well!" they are to jump inside their well.

EXTRA IDEA! While music is playing, let kids try to build a "well" with blocks, using the paper squares from the "Oh, Well!" activity. When the music stops, let kids crash down their well walls, and then clear the floor to start the game again.

Colorful Coats

 Before class, trace an outline of a simple coat onto a piece of paper. Then make a copy for each child onto 8½x11-inch sheets of white construction paper. Cut strips of colored tissue paper the same length as the coat outline, and write each child's name on a separate sheet of paper.

Give each child a coat outline, a paintbrush, and a small cup of water filled halfway. Set out the strips of colored tissue for kids to reach easily. Show kids how to brush the paper coats with the water then lay a strip of tissue on top of the watery coats. Have them continue until the coats are filled with colored tissue strips. Let the coats dry, then remove and throw away the tissues to view the beautiful water-colored coats. Remind kids that Joseph's dad gave him a beautiful coat because he loved Joseph.

Pharaoh's Dream Snack

 Set out bowls of different wheat and grain cereal pieces (such as a flavored Chex or Trix cereal) and chocolate or butterscotch chips. Set the bowls in a row (buffet style), and include a spoon in each bowl. Have kids wash their hands. Then give each child a resealable plastic bag to put the snack into. Let them measure and create "Pharaoh's Dream Snack" to serve to friends in class.

Everyone Is Special

 Honor a special family member each day this week. Give that person homemade gifts or eat a favorite meal from a special plate. At the end of the day, gather the family together, and talk about how well everyone did at not being jealous as Joseph's brothers were.

Clean It All

 Let your children help people clean their laundry by creating bags of laundry soap to give to your local laundromat. Set out a large box of laundry detergent one-cup measuring utensils, and resealable plastic lunch bags. Let kids place one cup of laundry detergent in each resealable bag. Remind kids that it was Joseph's job to measure out the grain and make sure everyone got a fair share of food similar to the way they are making small bags of soap to share with people at the laundromat.

Baby Moses

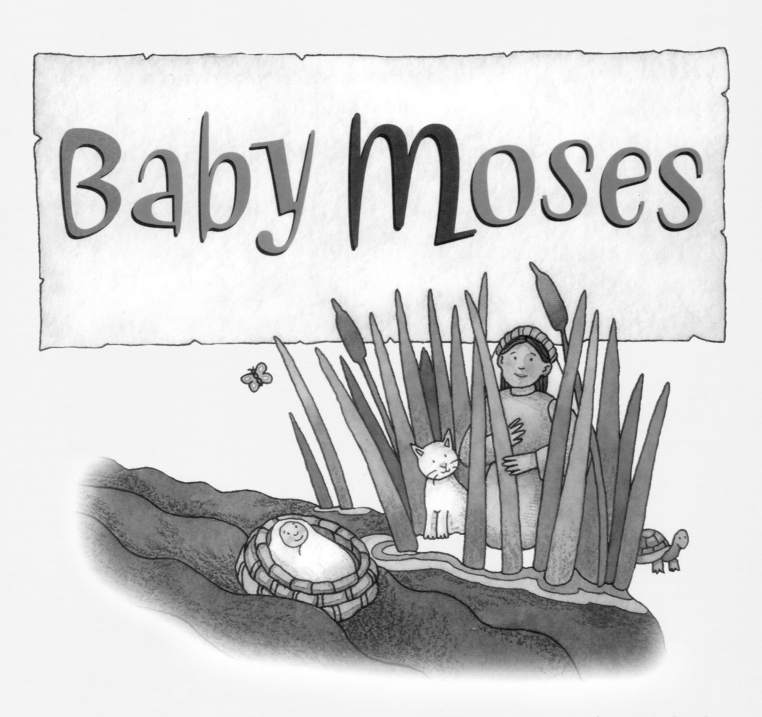

Exodus 1:1–2:10

Long ago God's special people, the Israelites, lived in the land of Egypt. There, a wicked king named Pharaoh made God's people work very hard. Pharaoh didn't love God and didn't love the Israelites! In fact, when he saw how many Israelites there were, Pharaoh made a terrible law that said the Israelites couldn't keep their baby boys.

The Israelites didn't want to follow Pharaoh's law. They knew it was wrong. One woman hid her baby boy for three months. But the baby grew and grew–pretty soon it was hard to hide him any longer!

So the baby's mother took a basket made from grass and covered it with sticky tar so it would float. She bundled up her baby boy and placed him in the basket.

Then she gently set the basket in the river, near the tall grass. Her daughter, Miriam, hid in the grass to see what would happen.

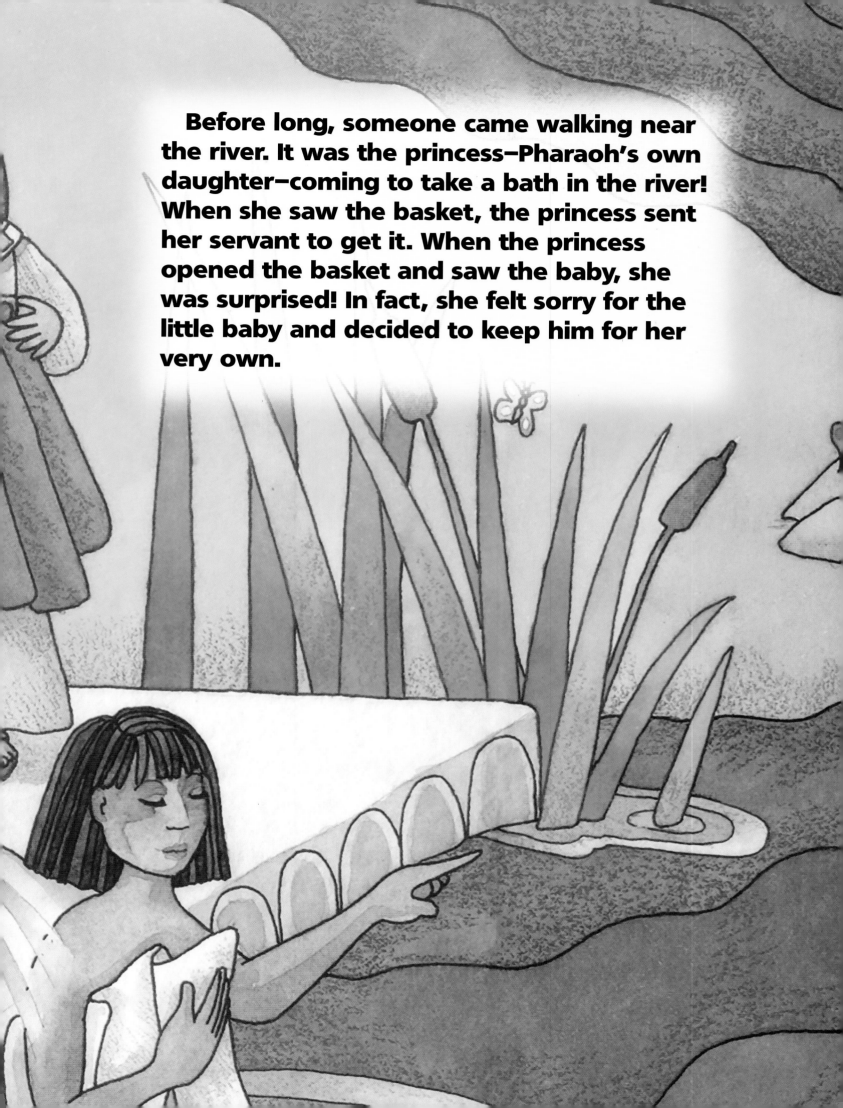

Before long, someone came walking near the river. It was the princess–Pharaoh's own daughter–coming to take a bath in the river! When she saw the basket, the princess sent her servant to get it. When the princess opened the basket and saw the baby, she was surprised! In fact, she felt sorry for the little baby and decided to keep him for her very own.

Suddenly Miriam stepped out from behind the tall grass. "Do you want me to go get someone to take care of this baby for you?"

"Yes, please," answered the princess. So Miriam ran and got her mother–the baby's own mother–to take care of him for the princess.

"Take good care of this baby," the princess said, "and I will pay you. When he is bigger, he will come and live with me in the palace."

The princess named the baby "Moses." When Moses got bigger, he lived in the palace just as the princess had said.

Hush, Little Moses

Here's a cute song your children will love to do with the motions. Sing "Hush, Little Moses" to the tune of "Hush, Little Baby."

Hush, little Moses (cradle arms and pretend to rock baby),
Don't be afraid. (Whisper, with finger to lips.)
God will protect you (point up)
Where you are laid. (Palms up.)

Hush, little Moses (cradle arms and pretend to rock baby),
Don't you cry. (Whisper, with finger to lips.)
God will protect you (point up)
While you float by. (Make wave motions with hands.)

Hush, little Moses (cradle arms and pretend to rock baby),
Don't make a peep. (Whisper, with finger to lips.)
God will protect you (point up)
While you're asleep. (Palms up.)

Hush, little Moses (cradle arms and pretend to rock baby),
Don't be alarmed. (Whisper, with finger to lips.)
God will return you (stretch arms out, then pull them in)
To Mommy's arms. (Hug self.)

Baby in the Basket

Remind your child that God was always with baby Moses and God will always be with him or her. Lead your child in singing and doing the motions to "Baby Moses" to the tune of "Ten Little Indians."

Mother put the baby in the basket (pretend to tuck baby into basket),
Mother put the baby in the basket (repeat motions),
Mother put the baby in the basket (repeat motions),
And set the boat afloat. (Wave and say goodbye.)

God kept Moses safe on the river (make wave motions with hands),
God kept Moses safe on the river (repeat motions),
God kept Moses safe on the river (repeat motions)
'Til the princess found him. (Pretend to hug baby.)

Baby Moses

Have family members sit together in pairs with their feet touching. Show them how to hold hands and rock back and forth as they sing "Baby Moses" to the tune of "Row, Row, Row Your Boat."

Baby Moses floats along
In a basket strong.
God is watching over him
As he floats along.

Let's Pray!

Pray With Feelings

Help family members identify feelings they see on your face as you say this prayer. Then say the prayer again, and let them express different feelings as they say the prayer with you.

**Dear God,
When I'm** [afraid, sad, lost, alone]**,
Please help me to remember
That you're my help.
Thank you for protecting me.
In Jesus' name, Amen.**

Hiding Prayers

Provide a large blanket or parachute. Tell your children that Moses' mother hid him in the basket so no one could see him. Remind them that God watched over baby Moses even when no one else could see him. Invite the children to hide under the blanket while you pray together.

**Dear God,
Thank you for always watching
over
us.
We love
you.
In Jesus'
name,
amen.**

New Ways to Pray

✔ Take your children to the church nursery to see the babies. When you return, ask the children to pray and thank God for all the babies he has created.

✔ Create a small bulletin board with pictures of people the children want to pray for such as the pastor, missionaries, or members who are sick and can't come to church. Cut out basket shapes from construction paper, and place them over the tops of the pictures to hide the people's faces similar to the way baby Moses was hidden in the basket. As you lead in prayer, allow each child to lift the paper basket to reveal the person's picture that is being prayed for.

✔ Take your child for a short prayer walk outside. Let your child touch the grass and thank God for making the tall grass that Miriam hid behind as she watched her little brother float to safety. Walk to a drinking fountain, and let your child thank God for the water God provided for baby Moses' escape.

also hid in the tall grass along the riverbank. When children finish their cattails, encourage them to "hide" behind them and pretend to be Miriam hiding in the tall grass.

Cattails

 Set out chenille wire, transparent tape, and cotton batting. Help your child tape cotton batting to the end of chenille wire to make cattails. Explain that cattails are tall grasses that grow at the edge of the water. Point out that Miriam

Hide and Take a Ride

 Let your children take turns being Moses. Set out a sturdy laundry basket or box, and have one child climb inside. Let a couple of other children cover "Moses" with a blanket or sheet, and then help you push Moses down the river (across the room). The other children can be Miriam hiding, parents praying, and the princess.

A Baby's Adventure

 Lead your children in the following finger play. Repeat the rhyme twice to help kids learn it.

Baby Moses went for a float (move hands up and down in wavelike motion)
In his little basket boat. (Cup hands together.)
Down the river, through the grass (pretend to push aside tall grass),
Sister Miriam watched him pass. (Shade eyes with hand.)

The princess heard him cry (cup hand behind ear),
And said, "What is that I spy? (Point in front of you.)
It looks like a little baby boy. (Pretend to hold a baby.)
He will be my pride and joy." (Clasp hands together and smile.)

Miriam knew just what to do. (Point to head.)
She said, "I'll find some help for you." (Nod head.)
So Miriam brought her mother 'round (beckon as if calling for someone),
And baby Moses was safe and sound. (Pretend to hold and rock baby.)

Baby-in-a-Basket Cookies

 Purchase pre-made sugar cookie dough, and follow the directions for preparation. Have your children wash their hands. Help them spoon out (or slice) the dough and place it on a prepared cookie sheet. Let kids press teddy bear cookies into the dough centers before baking. (Or after baking, kids could carefully press gummy bears into the cookies as they cool.) Bake the cookies as directed. Pray and let kids enjoy their "Baby-in-a-Basket Cookies."

Precious Little One

 Invite a new mom and dad to visit your home with their precious little one. Let your children congratulate the new parents and softly sing to the baby "Jesus Loves You" to the tune of "Jesus Loves Me." Lead the children in praying for the parents and thanking God for bringing this little one safely into the world.

EXTRA IDEA! Have your children make a "Basket of Blessings" (see below) to give to the new parents who bring their baby.

Basket of Blessings

 Let your child place small baby items such as baby lotion, baby bath soap, washcloths, baby wipes, and baby bottles in a basket, and let your child arrange their baby items in the basket. Use colored cellophane to wrap the basket, and then tie a large bow at the top. Give the basket to the next family in your church that has a baby or to your local women's shelter. Include a card that says, "God will take care of you," and let your child draw a face on the inside of the card and sign their names if they know how.

Ruth

Ruth 1-4

Naomi lived in the land of Moab with her husband, her two sons, and their wives. Then a very sad thing happened. Naomi's husband died, and so did her sons. Naomi decided to go back to Bethlehem, her hometown. "Go back to your own families," Naomi told her daughters-in-law. So Orpah said goodbye, but Ruth cried and promised, "Wherever you go, I'll go, too."

When Ruth and Naomi got to Bethlehem, it was the busiest time of year—harvest time. "I'll go into the fields and gather the leftover grain for us to eat," Ruth told Naomi. Naomi was too old to gather food for herself, so she was glad for Ruth's help. Ruth worked hard picking the grain. God watched over Ruth. But someone else was watching her too!

Boaz owned the fields where Ruth went to pick grain. One day Boaz saw Ruth in the fields and asked his men about her. They said, "She's Naomi's daughter-in-law. She asked if she could pick the grain we left behind. She's been working hard all day long."

Boaz was kind to Ruth. "You can work in my fields and no one will bother you," Boaz said to Ruth. "When you get hungry or thirsty, come share my food and water." Wasn't Boaz kind?

"Where did you work today?" Naomi asked. "In the field of a man named Boaz," Ruth answered. "He was very kind to me." "Praise God," Naomi rejoiced. "Boaz is a member of my family. Put on your best clothes tonight and go visit him. Lie down near his feet to ask for his protection." Ruth listened to Naomi and nodded. "I'll do everything you say."

That night Boaz slept outside to protect his grain. Suddenly he bumped into something and woke with a start. Ruth was lying near his feet! She said, "Please take care of me. We're part of the same family." Boaz said, "The Lord bless you. I will take care of you."

Everyone celebrated the day Boaz married
Ruth. What a feast they had! Naomi glowed
with happiness because God had given her a
new family. And before long, a little grandson
was born. Naomi, Ruth, Boaz, and little Obed
spent many happy years together loving each
other and God.

I'll Follow You

Your children will enjoy learning of Ruth's dedication and commitment to her mother-in-law. Sing this song to the tune of "My Bonnie Lies Over the Ocean" to learn of Ruth's words to Naomi.

**Wherever you go, I will follow.
Wherever you stay, I will too.
Your people will all be my people.
And your God, I'll worship with you.
Fol–low, fol–low,
I'll follow wherever you go today.
Fol–low, fol–low,
I'll follow you and there I'll stay.**

Ruth Hopes in God

Lead your children in singing and doing the motions to the following song to the tune of "The Farmer in the Dell."

Ruth picks the grain (pretend to pick up grain),
Ruth picks the grain. (Pretend to pick up grain.)
Ruth hopes in God (point up),
So Ruth picks the grain. (Pretend to pick up grain.)

Boaz cares for Ruth (pat friend on back),
Boaz cares for Ruth. (Pat friend on back.)
Ruth hopes in God. (Point up.)
Boaz cares for Ruth. (Pat friend on back.)

Boaz marries Ruth (hug friend),
Boaz marries Ruth. (Hug friend.)
Ruth hopes in God (point up),
So Boaz marries Ruth. (Hug friend.)

Ruth Was Faithful

Sing this song to the tune of "Frère Jacques."

**Ruth was faithful, Ruth was faithful
To Naomi, to Naomi.
She chose to bring home food;
She chose to marry Boaz.
God loved her, God loved her.**

Let's Pray!

Hope in God

Scatter enough drinking straws on the floor so that there is at least one straw per child. Remind your children that Ruth hoped in God and God helped her find Boaz's field where there was plenty of good grain for her and Naomi. Have children pick up the straws and pray, "Dear God, help us hope in you. In Jesus' name, amen."

God Is With Us

Create a simple path that includes these items in the following order: a shoe, a small bowl of wheat cereal or a stalk of wheat, and two rings tied together. Have the children follow you along the path as you lead them in this prayer:

Dear God (lead children to the shoe),
Help us to follow you as Ruth followed Naomi. (Hold up the shoe.)
Help us to serve others as Ruth served Naomi. (Walk to the cereal, and hold it up.)
Most of all (walk to the rings),
Help us to love you as Boaz loved Ruth. (Hold up the rings.)
In Jesus' name, amen.

New Ways to Pray

✔ If you serve children a snack made from wheat or other grains, remind them that the cereal is made from grains similar to the grains Ruth picked up in Boaz's field. Point out that Ruth took home the grain to make food for her and Naomi. Let the children thank God for the food he provided for them to eat.

✔ The next time you take your children on a journey outside, let them pray for God's safety and protection. Talk about the way God was with Ruth when she chose to stay with Naomi on their journey back to Naomi's home.

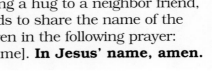

✔ Let kids share ways they can love others this week, such as giving a hug to a neighbor friend, helping a parent set the table, and assisting with dinner. Encourage kids to share the name of the people and what they will do to show their love. Lead each of the children in the following prayer:

Dear God, help me to [say the loving action and the person's name]. **In Jesus' name, amen.**

Let's Play!

God Made Grain

Before beginning, cut white paper into the shape of a large slice of bread. Cut brown construction paper the same shape but about one inch larger to form a frame for the artwork. Each child will need one of each size of bread shape.

Cover a table with newspaper, and have kids wear smocks to protect their clothing. Set out shallow bowls of three separate colors of tempera paint. Give each child a white bread shape and a wheat stalk. Show kids how to roll a wheat stalk in the paint and then use the stalk to roll, dot, or brush the paper to decorate the bread shapes. Remind kids that God provided wheat for Ruth to make bread for her and Naomi to eat.

When your children are finished, set their bread-shaped paintings aside to dry. Then glue their artwork to the brown bread shapes for kids to take home.

Separating the Grain

Before beginning, fold several paper fans from construction paper.

Set out a small bowl of large dry grains (such as barley), cotton balls, several pieces of brown construction paper. Explain to your children that part of harvesting in Bible times was to separate the grain from the stems. Workers tossed the mixture up in the air—the grain fell and the stems blew away in the wind.

Give each of the children a sheet of brown paper with a tablespoon of large grains and three cotton balls. Let kids blow the items on the paper to see which are light and will blow away with the wind. Some children may want to try dropping the items to see which of them land first. Tell the children that in Bible times, before people could make bread, they had to separate the heavy grains from the stems. Then they would smash the grains to make bread for their families.

EXTRA IDEA! Set up an area for a type of relay race. Place two long strips of masking tape parallel on the floor about five feet apart. Tell your children which line will be the starting line and which line will be the finish line. Create two to five lines of children behind the starting line. Give the first child in each line ten drinking straws. They will be the "planters." Tell the planters that when you say "go," they are to "plant" (drop) their wheat straws on the ground as they run to the finish line and then wait until all of the planters finish planting.

When the planters are finished, the next children in line (the "Ruths") will listen for the word "go," pick up as many of the straws as they can, and then run to the finish line. When each Ruth arrives, have everyone shout "Yea!" Kids can pick up or plant as many or as few straws as they want to before they cross the finish line.

Cookie Blessings

Invite grandparents from your congregation to your home or room, and let your children serve them a plate of purchased cookies or "Sticking-Together

Cookies" (see recipe below). Let your children also serve cups of milk to the visitors. Assign each child a "grandparent" to sit next to. Tell the grandparents that you're glad they came and allowed your children to serve and bless them as Ruth served and blessed Naomi during her life. Affirm them for the many years they loved, taught, and raised their children.

All–the–Time Rhyme

As you lead your children in the following responsive rhyme, remind them that Ruth loved Naomi all of the time and stayed with her. Before beginning, have each of the children practice finding a partner, linking index fingers, and saying, "A friend loves at all times" (Proverbs 17:17a).

Teacher: **A friend will love you when you're sad.** (Make sad face.)

Children: **A friend loves at all times.** (Link index fingers with friend.)

Teacher: **A friend will love you when you're mad.** (Make mad face.)

Children: **A friend loves at all times.** (Link index fingers with friend.)

Teacher: **A friend will love you when you do something wrong.** (Wave index finger back and forth.)

Children: **A friend loves at all times.** (Link index fingers with friend.)

Teacher: **A friend will love you all along.** (Hug yourself.)

Children: **A friend loves at all times.** (Link index fingers with friend.)

Sticking–Together Cookies

Have your children wash their hands. Give each child a paper plate, two vanilla wafers, a plastic knife, and about a tablespoon of the child's favorite frosting. Show your children how to spread the frosting on one cookie and place the other cookie on top of the frosting. As they make their snacks, encourage them to share ways they've "stuck" together in their families.

DAViD & Goliath

1 Samuel 17:1-50

David was the
littlest one in his family.
One day his father gave him
a special job to do.

David's father asked him to watch the sheep. While he watched them, David talked to God and made up songs to play and sing.

Sometimes wild animals attacked David's sheep.
But God helped David rescue his sheep.

One day, David's father asked David to take some food to his brothers. They were fighting battles in the king's army.

The king's soldiers were afraid. They were fighting a big giant. But David wasn't afraid. He knew God would help him.

David tried on the king's armor, but it was too big. So he went to the stream and picked up five stones. He'd fight that giant with his slingshot.

David's stone hit the
giant right in the head. The people
were so happy. They sang and danced
and praised God.

When David grew up, he became the king. He still sang songs to God, and he always trusted God to help him.

David, David

Lead children in singing "David, David" to the tune of "Ten Little Indians." During the verses, do the motions in the parentheses. During each chorus of "Children, children, God will help you," lead children in marching in place or around the room, or have them hold hands and walk around in a circle.

**Children, children, God will help you.
Children, children, God will help you.
Children, children, God will help you—just as he helped David.**

David, David pick up stones.
(Pretend to pick up stones and put them in bag.)
**David, David pick up stones.
David, David pick up stones.
You'll find them in the brook.**
(Wiggle fingers like a rippling brook.)

**Children, children, God will help you.
Children, children, God will help you.
Children, children, God will help you—just as he helped David.**

David, David swing your slingshot.
(Pretend to swing slingshot.)
**David, David swing your slingshot.
David, David swing your slingshot.
Swing it at Goliath.**
(Raise hands over head.)

**Children, children, God will help you.
Children, children, God will help you.
Children, children, God will help you—just as he helped David.**

See the Giant!

Let your children use washable markers to make a face on each of their index fingers. Tell kids to make one finger a Goliath puppet and the other finger a David puppet. Then lead them in singing the following song and the motions to "Twinkle, Twinkle, Little Star."

See the giant! Hear him shout
(hold up Goliath finger puppet, and pretend he's shouting),
**"Come and send a fighter out!
I don't want to fight a boy!
Send him home to play with toys!"
See the giant! Hear him shout,
"Come and send a fighter out!"**

"Hey, Goliath! My God's strong!
(Hold up David finger puppet, and pretend he's shouting.)
**He will help me right your wrong."
David raised and slung the sling.**
(Rotate David in a circular motion.)
Goliath fell and shook everything!
(Lower Goliath to side and shake hand from side to side.)
"Hey, Goliath! My God's strong!
(Raise David high in victory.)
He will help me right your wrong."

D–A–V–I–D

Sing the following song to the tune of "BINGO."

**There was a boy that fought for God,
And David was his name, oh.
D–A–V–I–D, D–A–V–I–D, D–A–V–I–D,
And David was his name, oh.**

EXTRA IDEA! Before beginning, make large letter cards spelling out David's name. Use 9x12-inch sheets of poster board or construction paper for each of the letters. As you sing the song, have children hold up each letter as it's slowly sung.

Let's Pray!

My Giant Prayer

Have family members think of problems in their lives that they want God's help with. Then lead them in the following prayer, letting them take turns filling in the prayer.

Dear God,
Thank you for helping us do great things! Help us to not be afraid of big problems such as...(have family members take turns saying things that are problems in their lives). **We're so glad that you make us strong like David!**
In Jesus' name, amen.

God Help Me, Too!

Lead the children in the following prayer. Remind kids that David trusted in God and God helped David defeat Goliath.

God, I trust you every day (put hands over head like sun shining)
To listen (point to ears)
To the prayers I pray. (Kneel and fold hands in prayer.)
I trust your help in all I do. (Hold up strong arms to indicate God's help.)
Help me do big things for you! (On "big," jump as high as you can.)
In Jesus' name, amen.

New Ways to Pray

✔ Bring in a toy suit of armor. Let your children take turns wearing the armor and praying spontaneously, asking God for help to be brave like David.

✔ Have family members sit in a circle for prayer time. Pass around a smooth stone. Let children each share one thing that makes them feel afraid. Then pray and ask God to help them be brave and trust God for victory.

✔ Ask kids to say the name of a tall person they know. Have the children thank God for creating tall people. Then encourage kids to show God's love to that person some time during the week. For example, kids could bring the person a candy bar or simply give him or her a hug.

Let's Play!

Slingshots

Cut two thirty-inch pieces of yarn and five to ten pieces of paper (5x5-inch) for each child. Give kids sandwich-sized resealable plastic bags. Show them how to punch a hole with a hole punch in each of the four corners of the resealable bag. Have each child hold the bag so that the opening is at the top, and then begin to thread a piece of yarn through both holes on one side of the baggie. Then repeat for the other side of the baggie. The yarn will hang loosely on each side.

Let kids crumple up the pieces of paper to place in the center of their slings. Then show them how to "sling" the wads at a pretend Goliath you've drawn on a chalkboard or white board. (Don't worry; it's a tough skill to master. Kids won't be able to hurl the "stones" hard enough to injure anyone.) Let them can count out five pieces of paper to place inside their slings for storage.

God Is Stronger Than Anything!

 Your children will delight in playing this tag game. Choose one child to be "Goliath" and one child to be "David." Tell the children that when you say the word "go," they will run from Goliath. If Goliath tags them, they must freeze into a statue. They can only unfreeze when David tags them and says, "God is stronger than anything!" Play the game for a few minutes, then choose a new David and Goliath, and continue playing.

Five Stone Cookies

 Mix together two cups of graham cracker crumbs and one can of sweetened condensed milk. Refrigerate the dough until ready to use.

Have your children wash their hands. Let each child form a handful dough into five small stone shapes and then roll each stone over a few chocolate chips. Remind kids that God provided the stones for David to defeat Goliath. This is a no-bake cookie, so your children can eat it right away.

"Someday I'll Be Bigger!"

 Have an adult-sized clothing and shoe drive. After the items are brought in, let each child in your class choose one item to keep for your dramatic play area. Choose one pair of women's shoes and one pair of men's shoes (the larger the better) to keep, and then give all the remainder items to your local shelter. Tell kids that David put on Saul's armor to fight Goliath, but it was too big for him to wear. Remind kids that God can use them no matter how small they are.

A Giant Adventure

 Gather your children into a circle. Ask them to repeat after you the following words and motions.

Goliath came to town. (March in place.)
He was looking for a fight. (Make a mean face and clench fists.)
God's people were afraid. (Knock knees together, and pretend to bite fingernails.)
Would things be all right? (Lift arms and shrug shoulders.)
David was not worried. (Wag finger back and forth.)
David was not scared. (Continue wagging finger.)
David trusted God when no one else dared. (Point upward.)
David took a stone (pretend to place stone in the palm of hand)
And put it in a sling. (Swing arm in big circles.)
Goliath hit the ground and made the earth shake and ring. (Bounce up and down.)
God used David to do a mighty thing (show strong muscles),
And that is why kids today still clap and sing! (Cup hands around mouth and shout, "Yea, David!")

EXTRA IDEA! After the story rhyme, have kids sing "Only a Boy Named David." You can find the song in *Wee Sing Bible Songs* and on its accompanying cassette (Pamela Conn Beall and Susan Hagen Nipp).

Big Talents for Little People

 Invite a few of the shortest adults you have in your church to your home or class, and let your children thank them for the "big" (important) talents they use for God. Have your children decorate big circles and add fabric ribbon to create "Big Awards" that they can give to the special visitors.

David and Jonathan

1 Samuel 18:1-4; 19:1-7; 20

Jonathan was a prince, and David was a shepherd.
But David and Jonathan were best friends. Jonathan
shared his armor with David.

Sometimes David came over to play his harp for Jonathan's father, King Saul. Usually King Saul liked David's playing, but one day he got mad and threw his spear at David.

King Saul wanted to kill David! Jonathan knew he had to warn his friend.

Jonathan found David and told David what King Saul was planning. He told David they'd always be friends, and he promised to help keep David safe.

That night at dinner, King Saul got even madder. He screamed and yelled at everyone and told them he wanted to kill David.

Jonathan made up a signal to warn David about King Saul's plan. Jonathan shot his arrows far into the field to let David know it wasn't safe for him to stay.

When it was time for David to leave, David and Jonathan
said goodbye. David was scared, but he knew God
would take care of him. David and Jonathan were sad,
but they knew they'd always be friends.

Where Is David?

 Have your children draw smiling faces on two round stickers and place each of the sticker faces on craft sticks to use as puppets. Tell children that David and Jonathan may have played Hide and Seek just as the children play with their friends. Lead your children in the following song and motions to the tune of "Where Is Thumbkin?" Have them begin the song with the puppets behind their backs.

Where is David? Where is David?
(Bring out Jonathan puppet.)
Here I am. Here I am. *(Bring David puppet from behind back.)*
Do you need my help, friend?
(Wiggle Jonathan puppet.)
Yes, I need your help, friend. *(Wiggle David puppet.)*
Run and hide. Run and hide. *(Wiggle Jonathan puppet, and hide David puppet behind back.)*

Ten Little Friends

 Lead your children in singing "Ten Little Friends" to the tune of "Ten Little Indians." Tell them to hold up their fingers and count the "friends."

One little, two little, three little friends,
Four little, five little, six little friends,
Seven little, eight little, nine little friends,
Ten little friends praise God! *(Raise hands and wiggle fingers.)*

Friends Stick Together

 Have your children stand and sing the following song to the tune of "The Farmer in the Dell." During the song, have each child turn to the person standing nearest and link arms so they are "stuck" together. Each time you repeat the song, have the kids turn to different classroom friends and link arms.

Friends stick together,
Friends stick together.
The Bible says that there's a friend
Who's closer than a brother!

Let's Pray!

Thanks for Friends

Have your children stand in a circle. Choose a child to stand in the middle. Lead the children in singing the following prayer to the tune of "Fre`re Jacques." Fill in the brackets with the name of the child in the middle. Repeat the song, giving each child the opportunity to stand in the middle. After the song, have each child turn to a friend and say, "Thank you for being my friend."

Thank you, God, for my friend
[child's name].
Thank you, God, for my friend.
Friends can help each other
Stick closer than brothers.
Thank you, God, for my friend.

Hand-and-Hand Friends

Bring out two washable stamp pads of different colors, white construction paper, and wet wipes for washing hands. Help each child find a partner to work with to create heart pictures. Show the kids how to partially close their fingers to make a half-heart shape. Let kids press the side of their fists onto a stamp pad and then down onto the paper. Have each partner use his or her opposite hand and do the same. Let kids make two pictures so they can each take a "Friendship Heart" home. Tell kids to wipe their hands, give their partners hugs, and say to God, "Thank you for being my friend."

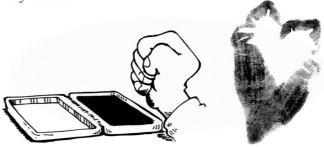

New Ways to Pray

✔ Have children sit in a circle and say the following prayer, completing the prayer with ways that they could help friends. **Dear God, thank you for my friends. I want to help my friend by** [child's thought]. **In Jesus' name, amen.** As each child finishes praying, he or she can hold the hand of the child seated to the right to indicate it's that child's turn. After everyone has prayed, point out that they are all linked together as friends.

✔ Have family members say the names of people who are their friends. Encourage them to name people who are older and younger than they are. Let each person spontaneously thank God for one friend.

✔ Have children sit in a tight circle. Cut a long piece of yarn that is the same size as your circle of friends. Place a bowl of large beads (one bead for each child) in the center of the circle. Ask children to name nice things people do for their friends. Then have each child pick up a bead, thread it onto the yarn, and say to God, "Help me be a good friend. In Jesus' name, amen." Continue around the circle, having children adding more beads and pushing them down. When the prayers and the "Friendship Rope" are finished, hang the rope up for all to see.

Let's Play!

Spin-a-Hug

Have your children sit in a circle with an empty soda bottle placed in the center. Tell kids that each of them will get a turn to spin the bottle and do something nice to the child that the bottle points to such as give a hug or a high five.

Friends Stick Together

Cut two gingerbread figures out of craft foam for each child. You can use a cookie cutter as the pattern. Write the children's names on the back of the foam people. Each child will also need one Velcro dot.

Let the children use markers to decorate the figures to represent Jonathan and David. Talk about how Jonathan and David were good friends. Then help each child attach a Velcro dot to the front of one figure's right hand and another piece of Velcro to the back of the other figure's left hand. Show the children how the friends "stick together."

EXTRA IDEA! Tear off a piece of wide masking tape for each child that will fit loosely around the wrist (clear packing tape also works well). Set out decorating supplies such as small scraps of colored tissue paper, flat beads, small gems, and small fancy pompoms. Place a masking tape band around each child's wrist with the sticky side facing out. Tell the children that they are to use the supplies to decorate the bracelets of all their classroom friends. Make it a fun game of Friendship Tag.

Helping Tickets

Create a list of ways your preschoolers could help others in small ways at home or at church. For example, fold five hand towels, polish a coffee table, wipe off dusty shoes, or pick up left over bulletins after a church service. Design a simple ticket that you can photocopy for the children to decorate.

Set out the tickets, markers, and stickers. Help your children make "Helper Tickets" for five-minute segments of help. Give the tickets to the parents, and tell them to deliver the tickets to people their children know, such as an older person, a sick person, relative, or family friend who the parents can depend on to call and "cash in" the tickets.

> Helper Ticket
> This ticket entitles_____
> to_____
> _____
> _____
> From_____

Hide-and-Seek Friends

Set up a box with a cover. The box should be large enough so a child can easily hide inside. Choose a child to pretend to be David to hide inside the box so King Saul won't find him. Give the rest of the children straws, and tell them to pretend they are Jonathan and the straws are Jonathan's arrows. Have the children form a circle and walk around the box holding their arrows and singing the following song to the tune of "London Bridge."

David, David, don't come out!
(Direct David to hide inside box.)
Don't come out! Don't come out!
David, David, don't come out! It's not safe. *(Stop and tell children to throw warning arrows over box.)*

David, David, come and play!
(Direct David to pop out of box.)
Come and play! Come and play!
David, David, come and play!
Everything's OK!

Pick up the straw arrows, and begin the Bible story game again.

Arrows of Friendship

Have children wash their hands. Serve pretzel sticks and small puffed triangle chips on paper plates. Show the kids how to arrange the triangle chips at the top of the pretzel sticks to create the arrows that Jonathan sent as a warning to David. Remind kids that God wants friends to protect each other. Pray and thank God for the snack, and then let kids enjoy!

Friendship Stars

Bring in a crown and a small step stool (or a small, sturdy wooden box or a sturdy chair). Drape a piece of fancy fabric over the top step to create an extra-special pedestal for standing on. Let your children take turns standing on the pedestal and wearing the crown. Let the other children say why they think that child is a good friend. Kids might say, "You help me," "You smile at me," or "You share your toys with me." After everyone has had a chance to be affirmed, lead the children in a giant class or family hug, and remind them that they are all good friends.

ELIJAH
& THE BIG SHOWDOWN

1 Kings 18:16-39

Long ago, a wicked king named Ahab ruled Israel.
King Ahab didn't love God—instead, he worshiped gods
made of wood and stone. God decided to punish King
Ahab. So God sent the prophet Elijah to tell the king,
"There will be no rain in your land for many years."

And sure enough, the rain stopped. God led Elijah
to a special hiding place where Elijah would be safe
from the angry king.

Twice a day, God sent ravens with bread and meat for Elijah to eat. When the brook went dry, God told Elijah to go to the town of Zarephath and stay with a widow and her son.

When Elijah found the widow, he said, "Please give me
a drink of water and a piece of bread."

"We only have a little flour and oil to bake bread,"
she answered. Elijah promised that God would make
sure she never ran out of flour and oil. And that's just
what happened! Every day the widow made bread,
but the flour jar never went empty and the oil jar
never went dry.

"Is that you, troublemaker?" King Ahab shouted to Elijah. "You're the one who's made trouble for Israel," Elijah shouted back. "You've disobeyed God and served idols instead. Now let's see whose god is more powerful. We'll both prepare meat to offer on an altar. You can pray to your god to light the fire on the altar. Then I'll pray to the *true* God. You'll see that God is powerful!"

The king's prophets shouted and danced from morning 'til night, but their god couldn't light the fire. There wasn't even a tiny spark. Their god was a fake!

Then Elijah built an altar to God. He piled on wood and meat, then dug a ditch around it. Guess what Elijah did next? He poured 12 jugs of water over the altar! How would it *ever* burn?

Elijah stepped forward and called out to God. "Answer me, O Lord," Elijah prayed, "so these people will know that you are God."

WHOOOSH! The altar exploded into flames! Snap! Sizzzzle! Hissss! The roaring flames burned up the wood, the meat, and the water. Even the stones melted into a smoky pile of ashes.

The people fell to the ground in fear and wonder. "The Lord is God! The Lord is God!" they cried. Hooray! God had won the showdown! The people learned that our powerful God is the only true God. Let's praise our powerful God. Hooray!

One True God

Lead your children in singing "One True God" to the tune of "Ten Little Indians." Do the accompanying motions for extra fun.

I will al-ways o-bey you, God.
(Reach hands to heaven.)
You're the one and only true God.
(Hold up one finger.)
I'll do what you ask me to, God.
(Nod head.)
You're the one true God! *(Hold up one finger.)*

Elijah always obeyed you, God.
(Reach hands to heaven.)
He knew you're the only true God.
(Hold up one finger.)
I will be just like him, too, God.
(Nod your head.)
You're the one true God. *(Hold up one finger.)*

I will al-ways o-bey you, God.
(Reach hands to heaven.)
You're the one and only true God.
(Hold up one finger.)
I'll do what you ask me to, God.
(Nod head.)
You're the one true God! *(Hold up one finger.)*

God Is True

Lead your children in singing the following song to the tune of "Ten Little Indians."

The prophets prayed, but there's no fire.
The prophets sang, but there's no fire.
The prophets shouted, but there's no fire.
Their god wasn't real.

Elijah prayed, and God sent fire.
Elijah prayed, and God sent fire.
Elijah prayed, and God sent fire.
Our God, he is true!

Oh, Elijah!

Give your children a chance to echo the joy of knowing that God is powerful. Lead them in singing the following song to the tune of "Frère Jacques." Sing each line, and then have kids echo each line back to you.

Oh, Elijah! *(Have children echo the line with hands to mouth as if calling someone.)*
Prophet of God. *(Echo and point upward.)*
Elijah knew God's power. *(Echo and show strong muscles.)*
Yes, he did! *(Echo and nod head.)*

Oh, Elijah! *(Echo and make calling motions.)*
Pray to God. *(Echo and fold hands.)*
Start the fire burning. *(Echo and rub hands back and forth quickly.)*
Praise the Lord! *(Echo and put arms in air.)*

Let's Pray!

Flour Prayer

Place a bag of flour, a spoon, and a jar in front of your children. Invite each child to come up and place a spoon of flour into the jar as he or she prays the following prayer to God.

Dear God, Thank you for always taking care of me as you took care of the woman and her son in the Bible. Amen.

A Stick and a Prayer

Set out brown sheets of construction paper for family members to roll up and tape together. Have them sit in a circle and place their construction paper sticks on top of each other in the center as if building an altar.

Say: **Elijah needed to show that his God was the real God. Elijah prayed and asked God to set the wood on fire. (You just made pretend wood sticks.) God answered Elijah's prayer, and the wood was all burned up along with all the water around it! All the people knew that Elijah's God was real and that they should serve him. Elijah's God is our God, too. We can also serve the one and only true God.**

Have family members pick up their "sticks," hold them high, and shout the following prayer to God.

You are real! You are real!
You are real! You are real!
We love you, God! Yea!

New Ways to Pray

✔ Help your children build a big square altar out of blocks. Then have the children stand around the outside of the altar holding hands (if their hands can reach). Lead the children in a short prayer, thanking God that he is the only true and real God.

✔ Tell your child every time he or she sees a bottle of oil to stop, remember the woman in the Bible, and thank God for taking care of his or her needs, too.

✔ Remind your child to pray for his or her friends who don't have dads. Ask God to take care of them as he took care of the boy in the story. Remind your child that God provides the friend's need for a father and is God, the Father, too.

Let's Play!

"Can" You?

Have a food drive throughout the month. Ask children and their parents to bring in nonperishable canned or boxed food items. Take the food to your local shelter or combine this project with the affirmation activity "Praise to the Giver," and present the food to the person that you and the children affirm.

Praise to the Giver

Place a long sheet of butcher paper on the floor, and give kids markers. Let children draw pictures of people being given food. When the children are finished, write, "Thank You" in large letters at the top of the paper.

Invite someone from a local food distribution center to visit your class. Present the banner, and thank him or her for the wonderful job the center does in providing food for so many people. Encourage the children to pray for that person before they leave. Remind kids that God provides food today as he provided food for Elijah.

Pretzel E's

This is a great craft for kids to make if you have access to an oven. Have the kids wash their hands. Let kids help you mix together the following ingredients to make pretzel dough. Measure 1½ cups of warm water into a large bowl. Sprinkle 1 package of yeast over the warm water, and stir until smooth. Add 1 teaspoon of salt, 1 tablespoon of sugar, and 4 cups of flour. Mix the dough just until it holds together, and then divide it into about a dozen pieces for the children. Let them knead their own dough for about 10 minutes.

Let each child make a snake-like shape and then form it into the letter E for Elijah's name. Remind the children of the woman that used her last bit of flour and oil to make bread for Elijah to eat.

Place the children's E's on a greased cookie sheet. Let the kids brush their pretzels with milk, melted butter, or beaten egg, and then sprinkle the pretzels with kosher salt. Bake in a 350-degree oven for about 12 to 15 minutes or until golden brown. Then let the kids enjoy!

Sacrifice Snacks

Before beginning this activity, have the kids wash their hands. Then give children plates and plastic knives. Let each child spread frosting on a graham cracker half. Let kids build make-believe altars by sticking a few miniature marshmallow "stones" to the frosting. Then have kids stack a few pretzel sticks on the top as "firewood." Have the children put orange and red candy sprinkles on their snacks to show that God burned up the sacrifice for Elijah. Thank God for the snacks, and let the kids enjoy their treats. Remind the children that we should serve God.

Feed the Face

Place a large vinyl tablecloth on the floor. Show the children how to draw Elijah's face on the back of a paper plate and then cut out the mouth from Elijah's face, leaving about a two-inch opening. Then show the kids how to tape a paper bowl under Elijah's face.

Give the kids about ten mini marshmallows or small snack crackers. Direct the children to spread out to give each other a little room, stand up, and drop the food into Elijah's mouth. Remind kids that God provided food for Elijah by sending ravens to feed him each day.

"Prophet-able" Power

Have your children form three groups, and tell them that they are going to act out the story of Elijah.

Give red, orange, and yellow crepe paper streamers to the Flame Dancers. Give large blocks to the Altar Builders. (If you don't have blocks, here's a way to make them: Stuff paper grocery sacks with crumpled newspapers, and slip another paper sack onto each one.) The third group will be the Shouters, Stompers, and Pray-ers. Also have an adult dressed in a robe pretend to be Elijah.

Direct each Flame Dancer to crouch down into a ball on the floor. Tell the Flame Dancers that they may only stand up and wave their "fire" streamers when someone prays to the *real* God. Direct the Altar Builders to build an "altar" around the Flame Dancers. Tell the third group they are to stomp on the floor, yell, and demand the Flame Dancers to make flames.

When nothing happens, have "Elijah" come to the Shouters, Stompers, and Pray-ers and tell them to pray quietly to the true God for fire. The group will kneel on the ground, and Elijah will say softly, "God, we know you are the real God, please send your fire so everyone will know that you are the real God!" The Flame Dancers will stand and do a fire dance and knock over the altar.

EXTRA IDEA! After leading the children in " 'Prophet-able' Power," have them sing "God Is True" to the tune of "Ten Little Indians." You'll find the words on page 87.

DANIEL
and His Friends

Daniel 1–3

Soldiers marched Daniel and his friends to a faraway city called Babylon. Many of God's people would be slaves in Babylon. But God was watching over them.

When they got to Babylon, the king chose Daniel and his friends to be his helpers. So they went to school in the king's palace. Every day they learned new things.

One night the king had a bad dream. He was very scared, and no one could tell him what his dream meant. But God was watching over Daniel and helped him tell the king about his dream.

Soon the king forgot about how God had helped him. He made a tall golden statue and ordered everyone to bow down and worship the statue instead of worshiping God.

Daniel's friends, Shadrach, Meshach, and Abednego, wouldn't bow down to the king's statue, so he threw them in a fiery furnace. But God sent an angel to watch over them there, too.

Shadrach, Meshach, and Abednego weren't even burned! Nobody could believe it. The king knew God had taken care of them. He ordered everyone to worship God from that day on.

Are You Dreaming?

Your children will enjoy learning this song about Daniel's ability to interpret dreams. Sing the song to the tune of "Frère Jacques." After your children have sung the song several times, let them skip around the room while singing to show how happy Daniel was when the king honored him for telling the meaning of the dreams.

God gave Daniel
A special job
To see dreams
And know what they mean.
God gave him the meaning
Of all the king was dreaming.
God gave Daniel
A special job.

Stand, Stand, Stand

Lead your children in singing the following song to the tune of "Row, Row, Row Your Boat."

Stand, stand, stand for God
No matter what you do.
Even when the going's rough,
God will help you through.

Daniel, Daniel

Have your children sit together in a circle. Lead them in singing the following song with motions to the tune of "Sailing, Sailing."

Daniel, Daniel,
Oh, stand up for God. *(Stand up.)*
Whenever you're afraid, just pray.
(Kneel down and fold hands in prayer.)
God will be with you. *(Hold hands*
with children on both sides.)

Daniel, Daniel,
Oh, stand up for God. *(Stand up.)*
Whenever you're afraid, just pray.
(Kneel down and fold hands in prayer.)
God will be with you. *(Hold hands*
with children on both sides.)

Let's Pray!

Roll-a-Prayer

Make a prayer cube by wrapping a square tissue box in plain paper. To represent ways we can pray, draw the following pictures on the sides of the cube: a stick figure with arms raised (praising), music notes (singing), a stick figure with hands together in prayer (asking), a heart (thanking), a sad face (being sorry), and an ear (listening). Then write the corresponding words under each picture.

Gather family members in a circle. Remind them that Daniel prayed throughout the day. Tell them that they can pray in many ways throughout the day, and show them the prayer cube. Tell

your family they will take turns rolling the cube and praying to God by doing the action that is facing up. Briefly explain each of the actions with the example actions as follows: To represent praising, raise arms and shout, "Yea, God!"; for singing, sing "Jesus Loves Me"; for asking, let a child pray for a need; for thanking, say, "Thanks, God, for [child's choice]"; for listening,

cup your hands around your ears and listen for ten seconds; for being sorry, bow heads and say, "God, we're sorry."

Let family members take turns tossing the cube and doing an action that corresponds to the word. You'll need to cue your children to do the appropriate actions for the first few turns, or let them make up their own actions to match the word. Remind family members that whenever they talk to God, they can be sure that God is listening to every word they say.

People of Praise

Before beginning, use masking tape to create four to six eighteen-inch squares on the floor in a corner of the room (or use a small carpet square to define a work space for each child). Place about ten blocks at each work space.

Remind your children that the king in the story of Daniel ordered all the people to worship a statue made from gold, but God wants us to worship only him. Explain to your children that they will build pretend people to praise God because each part of the "person" will represent one thing they can praise God for. Encourage children to thank God for their feet as they place the blocks for the "feet" in their work place. Then have kids each continue up the body including legs, stomach, chest, arms, hands, head, and facial features until children have praised God for every part of their bodies. Encourage them to pray, "Help me to stand tall and worship only you, God." The children can remove the blocks and build other structures, praising God for something different each time they place a block.

New Ways to Pray

✔ Bring in a kitchen timer. Let your kids take turns setting the timer, waiting for the buzzer, and then saying their prayers to God. Remind kids that Daniel prayed at special times during the day.

✔ Set out a numerical clock. Give your child a paper plate and markers to create and decorate a prayer clock of his or her own. Encourage your child to copy each of the numbers onto their plates.

✔ Take your children on a quiet walk to each room in your church. Be sure to include the kitchen, offices, and closets. Talk about how God is with them wherever they choose to pray. Encourage children to share how the room makes them feel. Kneel down and take turns praying a short prayer like "Thank you, God, for always hearing our prayers wherever we are."

EXTRA IDEAS! Instead of having kids draw the hands on the clock, create hands that can be copied onto construction paper and cut out. Give kids the cut-out clock hands, and help them attach the hands with paper fasteners to the center of their clocks.

Let's Play!

EXTRA IDEA! Create "fire" crayons for your children to use when they draw pictures of the fiery furnace. Collect old red, yellow, and orange crayons. Remove the paper wrappers, and break them into small pieces. Line the cups of a muffin tin with foil, and then fill each cup about halfway with mixed colored pieces of broken crayons. Bake in a preheated 300-degree oven for five to seven minutes. The crayons should melt just enough to blend the colors. Don't let them melt completely! Remove the tin from the oven, and let the crayons cool for at least thirty minutes. Peel off the foil before using the crayons.

Veggie-Print Aprons

Purchase inexpensive ready-made aprons from a craft store. Cut vegetables such as carrots, potatoes, celery, or bell peppers in half. Cut designs into the potatoes and carrots. Cover a table with newspaper, and set out shallow dishes of fabric paint. Encourage your children to use the vegetables to stamp designs onto their aprons. Tell your children that God made Daniel and his friends strong and healthy when they ate only vegetables (see Daniel 1:8-16). These creative aprons can be great gifts for Mother's or Father's Day!

Watching Glasses

Give your child two round or oval crackers. Help him or her spread whipped cheese on the crackers with plastic knives. Then place olives in the centers. Give your child a one-inch strip of licorice, and show him or her how to put the licorice between the two crackers to form "glasses." Explain that God doesn't need glasses to see us. As your child is eating the glasses, remind him or her that God watches

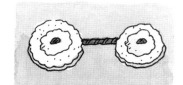

over us when we're scared, just as he was watching over Daniel's friends when they were in the fiery furnace.

Thank a Teacher

Invite your child to thank the assistant teacher or helper for teaching about God. Bring out a bag of Hershey's Hugs chocolates. Have your child think of something he or she learned about God that they can thank the teacher for. For example, your child might say, "Thank you for telling me that God loves me." When your child says "thank you," give him or her a Hugs chocolate to give to the teacher. Remind your child that when Daniel and his friends went to school in Babylon they had teachers that taught them important things also—how to read, for example.

Daniel Eats Healthy Foods

Your children will enjoy playing this version of Hot Potato while learning more about Daniel. Seat the children in a circle. Pass a potato around the circle while saying the words below. Say each line in a rhythmic fashion, and have the children echo the line. At the end of the rhyme, the child holding the potato will say, "Daniel ate potatoes, and he became strong." Use a different vegetable each time you play the game, and change the ending statement accordingly (for example, "Daniel ate carrots…"). After you play the game several times, snack on raw or steamed vegetable slices.

Daniel and his friends had to work for the king. *(Have children echo the line.)*
The king wanted them to eat everything. *(Echo.)*
Daniel said his people could not eat forbidden food. *(Echo.)*
The ruler thought that Daniel was being very rude. *(Echo.)*
Daniel said, "Let me eat food that is good for me." *(Echo.)*
And at the end of ten days, what a difference you'll see." *(Echo.)*
Daniel and his friend ate the food God OK'd. *(Echo.)*
Daniel was right—what a difference it made! *(Echo.)*
Daniel and his friends looked healthy and strong. *(Echo.)*
By obeying God, they couldn't go wrong! *(Echo.)*

Jesus Is Born

Luke 1:1–2:20

Long ago God told many men like the prophet Isaiah that Jesus would come and help them. They knew that Jesus was God's Son—the promised Savior.

At the right time, God sent an angel named Gabriel to a young woman named Mary. Mary felt afraid. Gabriel said, "Don't be afraid, Mary. God is happy with you. He's going to give you a special gift. You are going to have a baby, and his name will be Jesus. He'll be the Son of God—the promised Savior!"

The angel also told Mary that her cousin Elizabeth was going to have a baby, too. Mary loved God so much that she said, "I am God's servant. I believe you, and I will do whatever God says." Mary was so happy that she sang a beautiful song to God.

After the angel left, Mary went to visit Elizabeth. When she got to Elizabeth's house and said hello to Elizabeth, something strange happened. The baby that was growing inside Elizabeth jumped for joy! That's because Elizabeth and her baby knew that Jesus, the promised Savior, was going to be born!

Mary was going to be married to a man named Joseph. God sent an angel to tell Joseph in a dream that Mary's baby was God's special Son— the promised Savior—and that Joseph would name him Jesus.

Before Jesus was born, Mary and Joseph had to travel
a long way to a town called Bethlehem to be counted.
They became very tired, but they were also excited. God
had promised to send the world a Savior. The Savior was
coming very soon, and Jesus would be his name.

When Mary and Joseph came to Bethlehem, they tried to find a place to stay. But the innkeepers all said, "No room here! No room there! No room anywhere!" Finally, an innkeeper told them they could stay out in the stable with the animals. It was the only place he had.

So Mary and Joseph spent the night with the animals in the stable. There were cows and donkeys and sheep and doves. Then in the quiet of the night, God sent his promise! Jesus the Savior was born in Bethlehem! Mary wrapped baby Jesus in soft cloths and laid him on the hay in the animals' feeding box, called a manger. Just think how excited Mary and Joseph were when baby Jesus was born!

Well, God was excited too! A long time ago God planned a special way to tell the good news about Jesus' birth and tonight was the night. God sent an angel to some shepherds who were watching their sheep out in the hills near Bethlehem. The angel told the shepherds they could find Jesus the Savior lying in a manger wrapped in cloth. Then a huge group of angels began to sing and praise God! When the angels left, the shepherds ran to find Jesus. When they found him, they worshipped and praised God too. Jesus the promised Savior was born!

Going to Bethlehem

Lead your family in singing "Here We Go to Bethlehem" to the tune of "Mulberry Bush." As you sing the song, have family members skip or walk in a circle. When you repeat the song, turn and go in the other direction.

**Here we go to Bethlehem,
Bethlehem, Bethlehem.
Here we go to Bethlehem
To find a gift from God.**

Christmas Is Jesus' Birthday

Have your children stand up, hold hands in a circle, and sing the following song as they walk or skip around. This song is sung to the tune of "Camptown Races."

**Christmas is Jesus' birthday, doo-da, doo-da.
Christmas is Jesus' birthday. Oh, doo-da day!
He is a gift from God. He is a gift from God.
Christmas is Jesus' birthday. It's time to celebrate!**

Jesus Is Our Gift

Lead your children in singing "Jesus Is Our Gift" to the tune of "Jesus Loves Me." Encourage your children to do the motions.

Jesus was born one winter night.
(Pretend to rock baby in arms.)
Over head a star shone bright.
("Twinkle" fingers above head.)
Baby Jesus is God's Son. *(Hold one hand flat, then make fist with other hand and put it on top.)*
He's God's gift to everyone. *(Cover your heart.)*

Jesus is our gift. *(Point upward, then cover heart.)*
Jesus is our gift. *(Point upward, then cover your heart.)*
Jesus is our gift. *(Point upward, then cover your heart.)*
He is our gift from God. *(Cover your heart, then point upward.)*

Let's Pray!

A Caring Prayer

Gather family members in a circle. Hand your child a baby doll wrapped in a small blanket. Tell each member to gently pass the doll to the person sitting to the right and say a prayer. Have each person pray the following prayer as he or she passes the baby doll.

**Thank you, God, for
    sending Jesus.
We love you!
In Jesus name,
    amen.**

A Snuggle Prayer

Bring in a soft baby blanket that has an edging that is made from different material from the blanket itself. For example, it might have a silky edge. Allow children to touch the material to their hands, arms, legs, and faces. Discuss which piece is softest. Which one is prettiest? Ask children which one might have made a good blanket for baby Jesus to snuggle. Remind children how Mary wrapped her baby in a blanket to keep him warm. Then let kids again take turns holding the blanket saying:

**Dear God,
Thank you for sending Jesus to be
    born.
Amen.**

New Ways to Pray

✔ Gather your family, and crowd under a table, into a closet, or in another small area of your home. While you're there, pray a close-together prayer, thanking God for sending Jesus into a crowded world.

✔ Bring out any Christmas cards you received or are about to send. Encourage your children to pray for the friends of yours that need to know Jesus, the promised Savior. For your friends who are already believers, have your children pray that God will teach them something new about his love.

✔ Sit outside with your child on a clear, starry night, and try to find the brightest star. Join hands and pray that God will guide you closer to him each day.

Let's Play!

Angel Halos

Have your children make halos to wear. Set a roll of aluminum foil, scissors, and colorful ribbons on the table. Let your children tear long pieces of foil and twist them to fit around their heads. Have them wrap and tie lengths of colorful ribbon or sparkling chenille wires to the halos and let the ends hang down. As children work, talk about how the halos remind us of the shining and bright angels when they told the good news of Jesus' birth to the shepherds. When the halos are finished, encourage your children to wear their halos while they sing "Hark! The Herald Angels Sing" and proclaim the good news that Jesus is born!

God's Gift of Jesus!

 Have children sit in a circle on the floor. Designate one child to be the Angel. Have the Angel walk around the outside of the circle and tap each child on the shoulder. As the Angel taps each shoulder, have him or her say, "God's gift." After the Angel has gone around the circle, have the Angel choose one child to tap on the shoulder and say "Jesus" to. Then direct all of the children to stand up, hug each other, and shout, "Jesus is born!"

Baby Jesus Go to Sleep

 Help your children use washable markers to draw two eyes and a smiling mouth on each finger before you lead them in the following finger-play prayer. Repeat the rhyming prayer several times. Your children will enjoy learning the words and finger motions.

Five good shepherds watching their sheep. (Hold up five fingers.)
One saw the angel, and up he leapt. (Put other fingers down and hold up thumb.)
"Come," said the angel. "The Savior is here." (Beckon with other hand.)
Away went the shepherd without any fear. (Move hand behind back with thumb still up.)

Repeat the rhyme, holding up four, three, and two fingers, then only one finger. Finish with the following verse.

Five good shepherds standing in a row. (Hold up all five fingers.)
They all found Jesus and bowed down low. (Fold fingers down, making a fist.)
"We love you, Lord Jesus, we love you, we do. (Wiggle fingers excitedly.)
We'll tell our families and other people, too."

EXTRA IDEA! Arrange to take your children to an actual barn. Tell your children the Bible story. Then talk about how it looks, sounds, smells, and what it would be like to sleep in a barn.

Banana Mangers

 Cut peeled bananas in half and then in half again. Give each of the children a banana quarter and several shredded wheat mini squares. Let kids crumble their shredded wheat to make "hay." As they crumble the cereal, put a thin line of honey on each child's banana. Have children put their shredded wheat hay into their banana "mangers" and eat. As they enjoy the snack, remind them that the shepherds found baby Jesus lying in a manger.

Affirmation Wreath

 Take pictures of all the teachers and volunteers that help out with the children's ministry at your church. Use a juice lid as a guide to cut out all of the faces to fit inside the juice lids. Gather together juice lids for all the pictures.

Set out the pictures, the juice lids, and white glue. Let your children glue the pictures onto the juice lids and then bring the pictures to you. Arrange the pictures to form a wreath and then glue them all together using a cool temp glue gun. Place a pretty fabric bow at the top with a sign that reads, "Our gifts from God! Thank you for giving your best!"

Gift Gobblin'

 Have your children make gift snacks for a neighbor or another class. Have your children wash their hands before beginning. Let them spread softened cream cheese on graham cracker squares and decorate the tops with sprinkles and icing "ribbons" to look like presents with ribbons wrapped around them. Place the snacks on a large tray, and let kids or one of your volunteers deliver them. Then allow your children to decorate their own "gifts" as they wish. Remind them that Jesus is our gift from God— the promised Savior.

Jesus
IS WITH US

Mark 4:35-41; 5:22-24; 35-43; 10:13-16; and John 4:5-42

One day long ago, some parents brought their children to Jesus so he could bless them. Jesus' followers tried to send them away. They thought Jesus was too busy to see children. But Jesus said, "Let the children come to me!" Another time, Jesus told his followers that children are so important they have angels in heaven who watch over them all the time.

When Jesus was traveling through Samaria, he met a sad, lonely woman at a well. The woman didn't have any friends because of all the bad things she'd done. But Jesus wanted to be her friend, so he said, "Please give me a drink." As they talked, the woman realized that Jesus was the Messiah God promised.

When the woman realized who Jesus was, she ran back to town to tell everyone about her new friend. Lots of people came to see and hear Jesus for themselves. Jesus stayed and taught in that town for two whole days, and many people believed in him.

After teaching and healing people all day, Jesus was tired. So when he and his friends climbed into a boat to cross the lake, Jesus lay down and fell fast asleep. Suddenly, dark clouds raced across the sky and the wind began to howl. Huge waves crashed into the boat so it dipped and rocked and began to fill with water. The terrified disciples woke Jesus. "Lord, save us!" they cried. "We will drown!" When Jesus spoke to the wind and the waves, the lake became still.

When Jesus returned to Galilee, a big crowd welcomed him. Suddenly a man named Jairus pushed through the crowd and knelt at Jesus' feet. "Please come heal my daughter," Jairus begged. As Jesus and Jairus walked to Jairus' house, a man stopped them and said, "Your daughter is dead. Don't bother the teacher anymore." But Jesus said, "Don't be afraid. Just believe, and your daughter will be well."

Jairus *did* believe in Jesus. When they arrived at Jairus' house, Jesus sent away all the people who were crying. He said, "She's not dead, only asleep." And when Jesus took her hand, the little girl stood up. She was alive! Jairus wasn't sad anymore!

Jesus is with us today, just as he was with the people in these stories. Jesus is our forever friend who never leaves us alone. In fact, Jesus is with us right now as we read this book!

Jesus Said, "Be Still!"

 Create a few triangular-shaped "boats" on the floor with masking tape. Make the boats large enough for five to seven children to sit inside. Lead the children in singing and doing the motions to "Jesus Said, 'Be Still!' " to the tune of "Row, Row, Row Your Boat."

We're rowing our boats to sea.
(Pretend to row boat.)
We're rowing our boats to sea.
(Continue rowing.)
The wind is gentle as can be.
(Place finger over mouth as if saying "shh.")
We're rowing our boats to sea.
(Continue rowing.)

The wind is starting to grow. *(Rock back and forth and blow air.)*
The wind is starting to grow. *(Continue rocking and blowing air.)*
Lord Jesus is asleep below. *(Place head on hands and pretend to sleep.)*
The wind is starting to grow. *(Continue rocking and blowing air.)*

Lord Jesus, we're afraid. *(Place hands on cheeks and show fear.)*
Lord Jesus, we're afraid. *(Place hands on cheeks and show fear.)*
Wake up, wake up, and help us now! *(Pretend to wake someone.)*
Lord Jesus, we're afraid. *(Place hands on cheeks and show fear.)*

Jesus said, "Be still!" *(Place finger over mouth and say "shh.")*
Jesus said, "Be still!" *(Place finger over mouth and say "Shh.")*
The wind and the waves obeyed the Lord *(Pretend to freeze.)*
When Jesus said, "Be still!" *(Place finger over mouth and say "shh.")*

Jesus calms our fears. *(Hug yourself and rock back and forth.)*
Jesus calms our fears. *(Hug yourself and rock back and forth.)*
He makes our fears all disappear. *(Place hands in front of eyes.)*
Jesus calms our fears. *(Hug yourself and rock back and forth.)*

Jesus

 Gather children into a circle, and choose one child to be in the middle, who pretends to be Jesus. Tell the children to hold hands and stretch the circle out. Have the children walk in a circle around "Jesus" as they sing the following song to the tune of "Did You Ever See a Lassie?" Try creating two groups of children, and let them sing the different verses to each other.

Have you ever seen Jesus,
Seen Jesus, seen Jesus?
Have you ever seen Jesus
Turn children away?

He loves us and wants us
And cares for us all.
No, we've never seen Jesus
Turn children away!

Ring Around the Well

 Have your children stand up and hold hands with one another. Have them move around in a circle, singing the following song to the tune of "Ring Around the Rosie."

Ring around the well.
I am thirsty, can't you tell? *(Pretend to dip cup into water and drink.)*
Water, water,
Let's drink it from the well. *(Hug yourself.)*

Let's Pray!

Down the Drain

Have your child stand at a sink with you and tell about some things that may frighten him or her. Stop the drain, and let your child run a little water into the sink for each fear. Ask how he or she can give that fear to Jesus. Then say the following prayer together, mentioning a fear in the first line of the prayer. For example, the first line may be, "When in the dark I have a fear," or "When we have a thunderstorm and I have a fear."

Dear God, When [name a source of fear] **I have a fear, Help me feel you standing here. Amen.**

Unplug the drain so your child can watch the "fears" go down the drain. During the week, help him or her brainstorm about solutions for those fears.

Prayers for the Children

Purchase stickers of Jesus from your local Christian bookstore. Use an instant camera, and help each child take a picture of the class. Set out magazines, glue, construction paper, scissors, and fine-tip markers. Then help children cut or tear pictures of children out of the magazines and glue them onto the construction paper. Next have kids glue their photos in the center and place the Jesus sticker on the edge of their photo. Encourage children to tape the pictures next to their beds as reminders that Jesus loves children and wants them to freely come to him.

New Ways to Pray

✔ Encourage family members to thank Jesus for being their living water each time they pour themselves a drink.

✔ Fill a plastic soda bottle a third of the way with water. Add one drop of blue food coloring and a few sprinkles of glitter to the water. Place the lid tightly on the bottle. Pass the bottle around during prayer time, and let your children shake the bottle, making "stormy waves." As each child shares, have him or her tell God one fear. Let the child watch the waves in the bottle calm down and then tell God thank you before passing the storm bottle to the next child.

✔ Have your children sit in a circle, and place a picture of Jesus in the center. Give children each a toy figure or elf cookie that will represent them. One at a time, have the children walk their figures to Jesus and pray, "Thank you, Jesus, for wanting me with you."

Let's Play!

Jesus Is With You!

To help your children understand more about the way Jesus is always with them, give each child at least ten Jesus stickers. Choose one of the children's favorite praise songs to play in the background as they affirm each other and give away their stickers. Tell the children that when you start the music they are to go quickly to class friends, place Jesus stickers on them, and say, "Jesus is with you!" When the music stops, they are to freeze. As the children play, start and stop the music quickly, only allowing them to place two or three stickers on friends at a time. At the end, have everyone join together in a large group hug, look at each other, and shout, "Jesus is with you!"

Sock Doll

Show your child how to make a sock doll that he or she can use to re-enact either Bible story in this lesson. Some suggestions for Bible characters that your child might like to make are Jesus, the woman at the well, Jairus, and Jairus' daughter. Show your child how to put fabric stuffing down into a tube sock and then use chenille wires to wrap around the upper and lower body to create the arms and legs. At the top of the head, about one inch from the end, place a rubber band, and then turn the end of the sock down onto the head to create a helmet for Jairus, the soldier. Give your child wiggly eyes to glue onto the face and markers to create the nose and mouth for his or her puppet. Encourage your child to retell the Bible story to other family members or friends. Older children may enjoy working together to tell the Bible story.

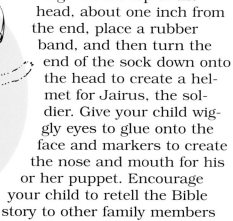

EXTRA IDEA! Write simple, two-puppet skits that an adult can narrate and the children can follow along, acting out the characters of the Bible stories with their sock puppets. Practice a few times, and then invite a younger class to join you. Let the children use their puppets to tell the Bible story to the other children.

Quiet, Storm! Quiet!

This is an extremely active game as the children pretend to be the storm that Jesus calms.

Beforehand, put a strip of masking tape on the floor of the room or use a couple of jump-ropes for outside on the playground, about ten to fifteen feet long. Gather three half-sheets of newspaper for each child.

Form two groups of children, and have one group stand on one side of the masking tape and one group on the other side. Tell your children they will be playing a game about Jesus calming the stormy sea. As you retell the story, have kids make stormy noises by loudly crumpling their newspaper into three little "rain" balls, and then have kids set their rain balls down on their side of the line. Pick a child to be "Jesus," and have him or her lay down at one end of the line and pretend to sleep. When you tell your children about the storm, have them throw the rain balls back and forth across the line. After a little while, wake "Jesus" up. Jesus will stand up and shout, "Quiet! Be still!" Your children will stop throwing the rain balls. Repeat the story choosing a new Jesus each time.

A Windy Snack

Wash and dry small lids for your children to use as boats. Have kids wash their hands or use wet wipes. Give each child a straw and a shallow bowl filled with milk. Let kids place their teddy bear cookies inside the small lids, and then place the lids in the bowl of milk to re-enact the Bible story. When the storm comes up, have kids slowly blow their "boats" with their straws across the milky sea, tell the storm to stop, and then enjoy their snack.

Refreshing Water

Toward the end of your church's worship service, have a volunteer set up a table with two to four large water pitchers or coolers with spouts. Fill the pitchers with ice water, and set out cups. Have printed signs taped to the pitchers that read, "Jesus is our living water!" (If possible, have about one water cooler for every two to five children.) When the service is over, let the children serve the church people cups of cool, refreshing water. Remind your children that Jesus told the woman at the well that he could give her living water so she would never thirst again.

The Good Samaritan

Luke 10:25-37

Jesus once told a story about a traveler who was walk-ing along a road one bright, sunny day. Suddenly rob-bers jumped on the man and pushed him to the ground! There were too many robbers, and the man couldn't protect himself. The robbers stole everything the man had and left him hurt and bleeding on the road.

Ooh, thought the man. I'm hurt and I can't get up! Surely someone will come and help me.

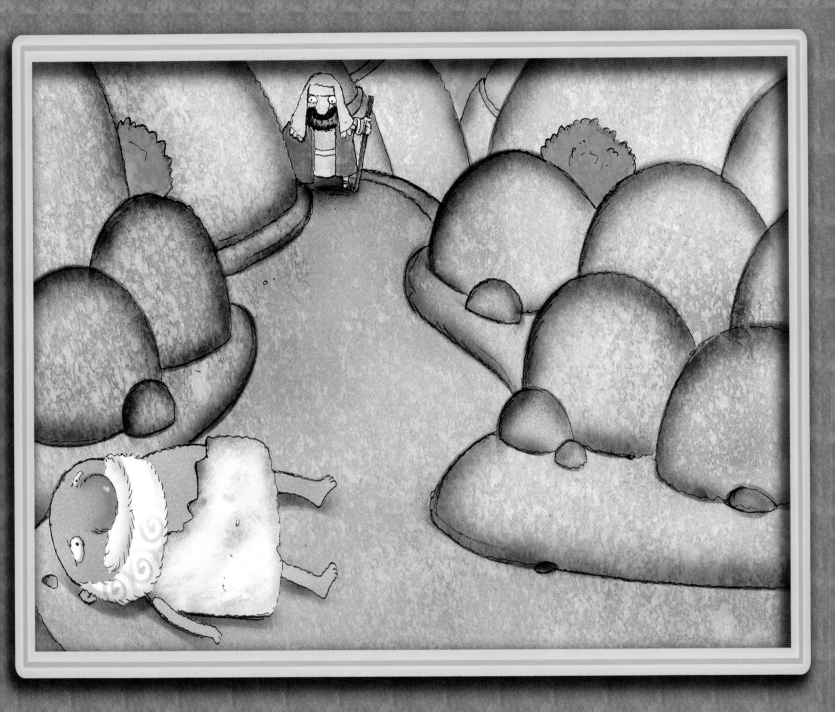

Soon the man heard footsteps coming along the road. He could hear them coming closer. The hurt man just lay there on the road. The footsteps got louder and louder as the second man came closer.

"Ooh," the man said. He was too weak to call out. It was a priest! *Oh surely, he'll stop,* thought the hurt man. But when the priest came to the hurt man...

He didn't stop! He walked right by! The priest walked on by with his head held high! The hurt man just lay on the road.

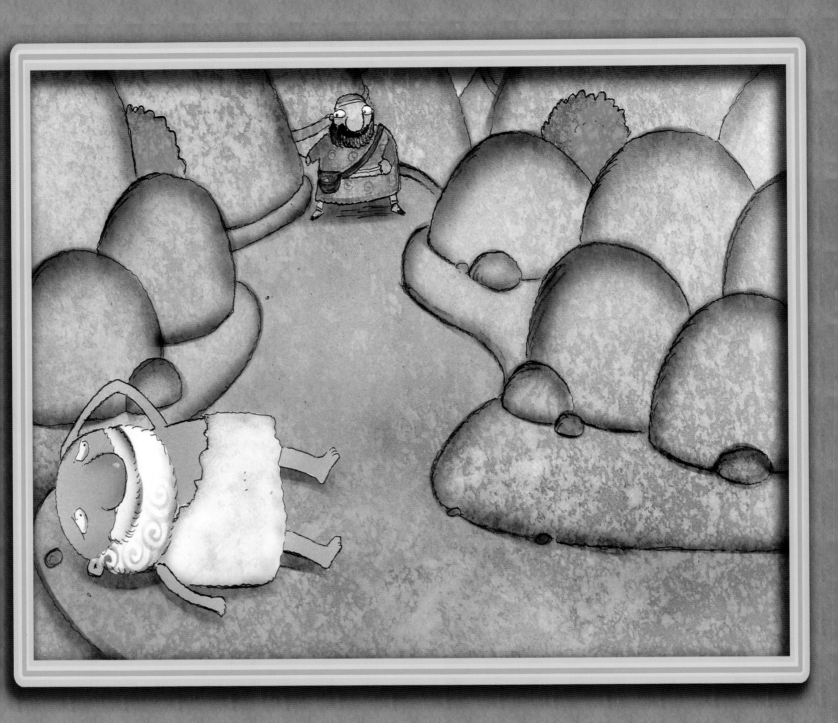

After a while, he heard more footsteps coming. They came closer and closer and got louder and louder.

The hurt man could now see that it was a Levite. *A man who loves God as I do,* thought the hurt man. *Surely he'll stop.* "Ooh," the man said. But when the Levite came to the hurt man...

He didn't stop! He walked right by! The Levite walked on by with his head held high! The hurt man just lay on the road.

After a long while, he heard more footsteps coming. Louder and closer, closer and louder the footsteps came! *It's a man from Samaria–a man who doesn't like Jewish men like me,* thought the man on the road. *Surely, he won't stop to help.* "Ooh," the man said. When the Samaritan came to the hurting man . . .

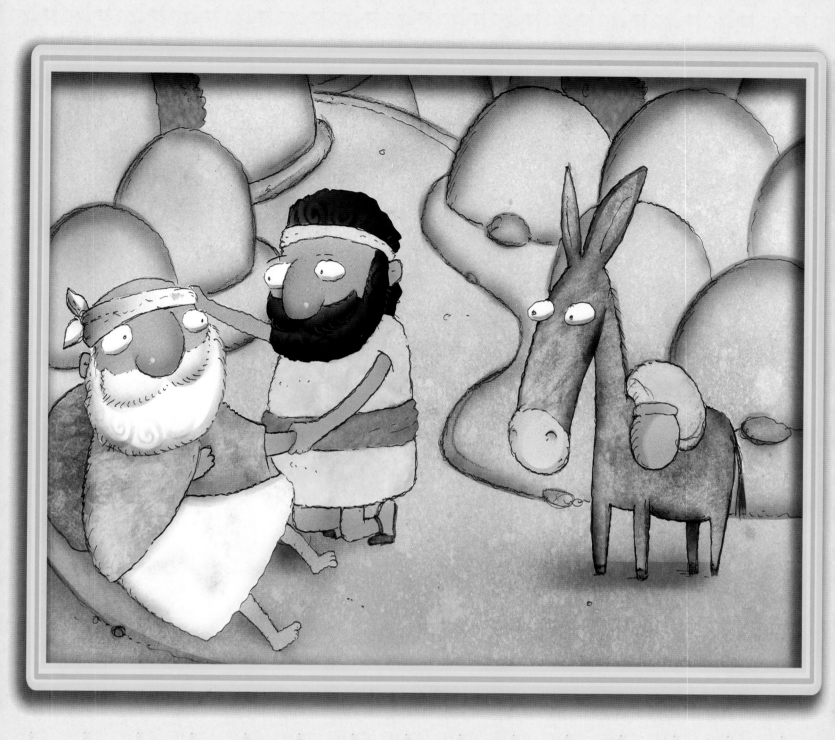

He stopped! He didn't walk right by! The Samaritan stayed right by his side! The Samaritan felt sorry for the hurt man. The Samaritan put medicine on his wounds to make him feel better. Then the good Samaritan put bandages on the hurt man to stop the bleeding.

The good Samaritan lifted the hurt man onto his donkey and took the man to town. He took the man to an inn and asked the innkeeper to take care of the hurt man. The good Samaritan even gave the innkeeper money to take care of him. The good Samaritan was God's helper that day. You can be God's helper, too!

If You Want to Care for Someone

Sing the following song to the tune of "If You're Happy and You Know It."

If you want to care for someone,
give a hug.
If you want to care for someone,
give a hug.
If you want to show you care,
God's love is good to share.
If you want to care for someone,
give a hug.

If you want to care for someone,
show a smile.
If you want to care for someone,
show a smile.
If you want to show you care,
God's love is good to share
If you want to care for someone,
show a smile.

If you want to care for someone,
pat a back.
If you want to care for someone,
pat a back.
If you want to show you care,
God's love is good to share.
If you want to care for someone,
pat a back.

One, Two, Three

Sing this song to the tune of "Row, Row, Row Your Boat."

One, two, three smart men
Walked along a road.
They saw a man lying there
Hurt from head to toe.

Only the Samaritan—
As kind as he could be—
Stopped and helped the hurting
man
And took him to safe-ty.

You and I can be so kind
To people everywhere.
We only need to stop and look
And take the time to care.

Care, Care for One Another

Lead your children in singing this song to the tune of "Climb, Climb Up Sunshine Mountain."

Care, care for one another;
God commands us to.
Care, care for one another;
That's what we should do.
Ask, ask for God to help you;
Look to him on high.
Care, care for one another—
You and I.

Let's Pray!

Care Prayer

Tell your children that you'll say a prayer then you'll pause in the middle so that they can tell ways to show kindness or care for others. Kids might say things such as "Help my mom with chores" or "Be quiet when my baby sister is sleeping." Go around the circle in one direction. Ask children each to hug the next child as a cue for that child to share next.

Dear God,
We love you so much, and we thank you for sending Jesus to show us how we can care for others. Help us to find new ways every day to care for others, such as (Ask kids each to share and then hug the next child.) **We're so glad that you love us so much. Help us to share your love with others.**
In Jesus' name, amen.

The-One-Who-Cares Prayer

Gather your children into a circle. Remind them that Jesus wants us to care for others. Say the following rhyming prayer and do the motions together.

Help me, Jesus, to be kind (point to heaven on "Jesus")
And care for others when I find (point to others)
That they have need of love and prayers. (Fold hands in prayer.)
Help me be the one who cares. (Point to yourself.)
In Jesus' name, amen.

New Ways to Pray

✔ Have your child make a small red dot on his or her hand with a red washable marker to represent a "hurt." Give your child a bandage, and let him or her bandage other family members' hurts. As your child places the bandages on the pretend wounds, have him or her say, "Dear Jesus, Help me be kind today."

✔ Give your child a drop of instant hand sanitizer as he or she thanks God for his care, like the way the Samaritan cared for the hurting man on the road.

✔ Have each child think of a friend or person he or she wants to pray for. Using a permanent marker, write that person's name on the outside of an adhesive bandage and give the bandage to the child as a reminder to pray for that person.

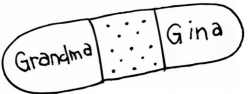

Let's Play!

A Friend in Need

 Show your children how to make the hurting man from the Bible story. Give each child a plate with one piece of lunchmeat (such as salami or bologna), one slice of cheese, one small round cracker, and two pretzel sticks. Demonstrate how to roll up the slice of meat and push a pretzel stick into each side of the roll, then place the cracker at the top of one end of the roll and place the cheese "blanket" over the man's body. Have each of your children show kindness by giving the snack to the child on the right.

Stethoscopes

Before beginning, cut paper towel tubes into two-inch lengths and yarn into twelve-inch lengths. Each child will need one of each. Place the yarn, the two-inch sections of paper tubing, and hole punches on a table. Have children punch holes on opposite sides of their tubes. Help children thread the yarn through the holes and tie the ends of the yarn together. Let children decorate their "stethoscopes" with stickers and markers and slip the stethoscopes over their heads. Have each child place the stethoscope up to one ear. Encourage kids to find partners and listen to each other's heartbeats. As children listen, tell them that a doctor listens to our hearts when we're sick or hurting. Remind the children that we can help others who are hurt because we care for them as the good Samaritan cared for the hurting man on the road.

EXTRA IDEA! Let kids make "bandages of kindness." Place 2x6-inch pieces of masking tape sticky side down on the table (one in front of each child). Set out glitter crayons for children to decorate the outside of the bandages. Give each child four cotton balls, and have him or her place the cotton balls in the center of the sticky side of the masking tape. Help kids form pairs and place them on each other's pretend "owies."

Be Kind to Others!

Have your children stand up and form a circle. Choose a child to lie on the floor in the middle of the circle and pretend to be the hurt man along the road. Give one child in the circle a small towel. Lead the children in singing the following song to the tune of "The Farmer in the Dell." While they sing, have the children pass the towel around the circle. At the end of the song, whoever is holding the towel will run into the center, place it over the hurt man, and shout, "I'll be kind!"

**A man lies on the road,
A man lies on the road.
What will you do to help the man?
A man lies on the road.**

Good Sam

Demonstrate how to make a marshmallow man. Push one end of a pretzel stick into a large marshmallow that will represent the body of the man. To make the man's head, push a smaller marshmallow onto the other end of the pretzel stick. Tell the children not to each their marshmallow men yet because they will use them to help tell the Bible story.

Say: **A man asked Jesus, "Who is my neighbor?" So Jesus told this story.** (Hold marshmallow man up.) **This man was walking down the road when some bandits came along and beat him up. He lay hurt in the road.** (Lay man down in palm of other hand.)
A priest walked by and saw the man who was hurt. (Have each child turn to a neighbor. Have one child pretend his or her marshmallow man is the priest and the partner's marshmallow man is the wounded man.) **He saw the man who was hurt, but he kept on going.**
Another man came by. (Ask children to walk their marshmallow men by their partners' wounded men again.) **He saw the man who was hurting, but he kept on walking.**
Then a good man came by. The Bible calls him a good Samaritan. Let's call him Good Sam. (Ask each child to pretend the marshmallow man is Good Sam.)
He saw the wounded man, and he took a deep breath in surprise! (Have the children gasp loudly.) **He helped the man. Good Sam carried the hurt man to safety. He took him to an innkeeper. Good Sam gave the innkeeper money to feed the hurt man and care for him.** (Ask all the children to say, "Take care of him for me!")
God loves us all, and he wants to take care of us the way Good Sam took care of his neighbor, the man who was hurt.

Zacchaeus

Luke 19:1-10

ZACCHAEUS was rich—very, very rich. His job was to collect money for taxes from everyone in town. But Zacchaeus took more money than he was supposed to and kept the extra money for himself! The people didn't like Zacchaeus one bit.

One day Jesus came to town. Everybody wanted to see Jesus because they'd heard how he could heal the sick and make blind people see. Zacchaeus wanted to see Jesus, too, but he was too small to see over the crowd.

So Zacchaeus ran ahead of the crowd and climbed up in a tree. As Jesus came closer and closer, Zacchaeus' heart began to pound. Then Jesus looked right at him and said, "Zacchaeus, hurry and come down! I must stay at your house today."

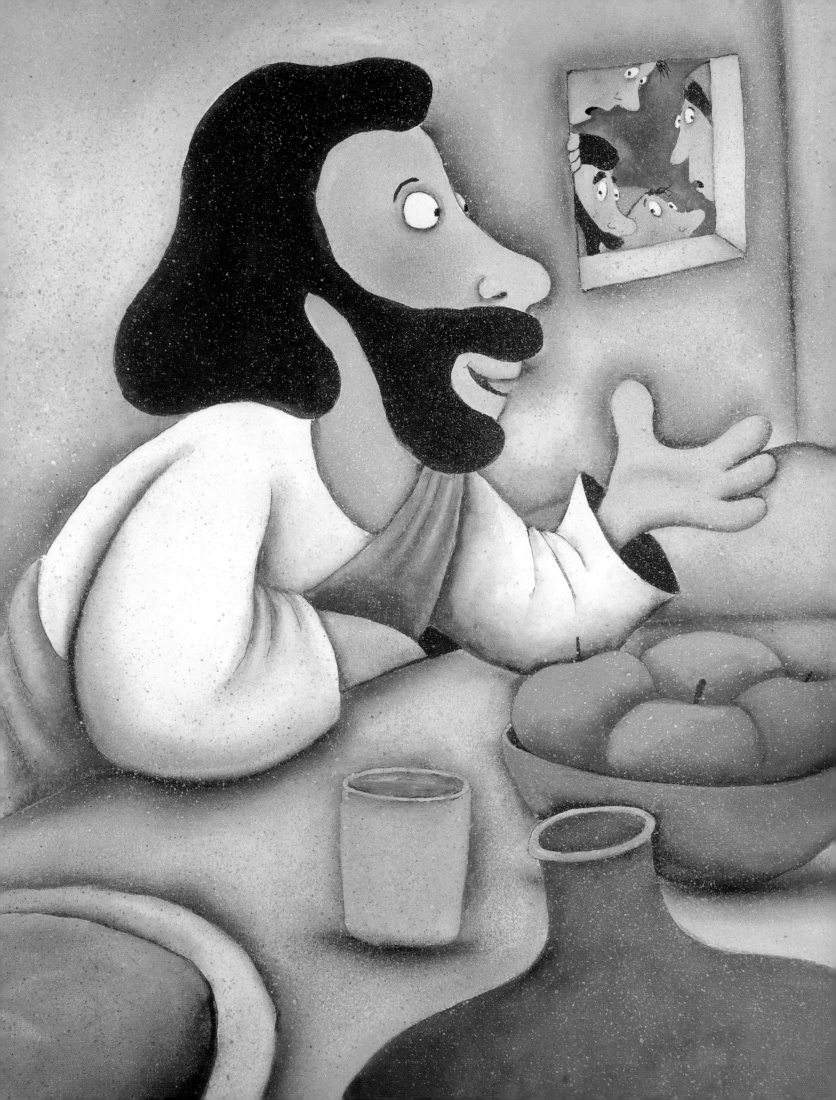

Zacchaeus was so excited! Jesus wanted to come to his house! He hurried down from the tree and ran right home to prepare a meal for Jesus. The people in the crowd began to mumble and complain. They didn't like Zacchaeus, and they didn't want Jesus to go to his house! But Jesus knew that Zacchaeus was sorry for all the bad things he'd done. God's love changed Zacchaeus, and he promised to give back all the money he'd taken.

Right away Zacchaeus started giving people back the money he'd stolen. If he had taken one bag of coins, he gave back four! The people were amazed and happy that Zacchaeus had learned to do what's right. Zacchaeus was glad, too.

Zacchaeus

 Lead children in the song and motions for "Zacchaeus Was a Wee Little Man."

Zacchaeus was a wee little man
(hold hand at waist level, and show how little he was),
And a wee little man was he.
He climbed up in a sycamore tree
(pretend to climb a tree)
For the Lord he wanted to see.
(Place hand on forehead and look around.)
And as the Savior passed that way *(walk fingers up forearm),*
He looked up in the tree. *(Place hand on forehead and look up.)*
And he said, "Zacchaeus, you come down! *(Point up, then point down.)*
For I'm going to your house today *(walk in place),*
For I'm going to your house today.

Zacchaeus Song

 Children will enjoy this musical version of Zacchaeus' story. Sing it to the tune of "I'm a Little Teapot."

I'm Zacchaeus, short and small.
(Pat the air near the ground.)
I want to see Jesus, but the people are too tall. *(Pat the air above your head.)*
Maybe if I climb that sycamore tree *(pretend to climb),*
I'll see Jesus and he'll see me.
(Point away from yourself, then point to yourself.)

I'm Coming to Your House

 Form a circle. Ask one child to pretend to be Jesus and stand in the center. Have the rest of the group hold hands and walk around in a circle as they sing "I'm Coming to Your House" to the tune of "The Farmer in the Dell."

"I'm coming to your house,"
I'm coming to your house."
Jesus told Zacchaeus,
"I'm coming to your house."

Direct "Jesus" to select someone to be "Zacchaeus," and have that child come to the center. Help the children in the center act out one way to show kindness such as giving a hug. Then send both children back to the circle, and choose a new Jesus. Repeat the game until everyone has had a turn to be Jesus or Zacchaeus. Remind the children that Zacchaeus learned to be kind and Jesus wants us to be kind too.

Let's Pray!

Treetop Prayer

If your home has a large tree on the premises, take your child outside to lie down around the trunk. Encourage your child to look up into the branches. Tell the Bible story, and ask him or her to imagine looking up and seeing Zacchaeus in the tree! At the end, hold hands and pray, telling Jesus how much you love him.

A Climbing Prayer

Bring a small step stool to class to represent the tree Zacchaeus climbed to see Jesus.

Hold the "tree" steady as you invite each child at a time to climb to the top and say a prayer, thanking Jesus for wanting to be a friend, the way he was to Zacchaeus. After each child has had a turn to pray, invite everyone to say in unison, "In Jesus' name, amen."

EXTRA IDEA!
Tape a few branches or construction paper leaves to the sides of the step stool to make it look more like a tree.

New Ways to Pray

✔ Bring out one lunch bag with a small cracker inside for each child. Have the children sit in a circle, and begin to pass the bag. As each child receives the bag, have him or her reach inside, pull out one cracker, and tell about a day spent with Jesus if he came to their house.

✔ Have family members pretend to be very small and crouch down into a ball with his or her hands folded. Let each person take turns thanking God for the size he or she is. Then have your family stand up and stretch.

✔ During snack time, have your children take turns inviting one friend to eat with them the way Jesus invited himself to Zacchaeus' home. Before your children eat their snack have them pray together, thanking God for caring about them and providing their snack.

Let's Play!

Coin Purses

Distribute paper plates, and show children how to fold in the opposite edges of the plate about an inch. Then show kids how to fold the plate in half to make the shape of a coin purse. Staple the sides of each plate, near the bottom, and then punch two holes in the top edges. Help each child string a length of yarn through the holes. Be sure the yarn is long enough to allow children to pull the coin purses open. Allow children to decorate their coin purses with crayons, markers, and stickers. As children work, review how Zacchaeus collected too much money from people, then gave back four times as much as he took. Remind them that Jesus wants us to be sorry when we do wrong.

Sitting in a Tree

 This singsong rhyme is great fun! The children do the actions while you recite the verse.

Poor little Zacchaeus, small as he could be. (Hold hand up and point to pinkie.)
Wanted to see Jesus but was too short to see. (Shrug shoulders with palms up.)

A thought came to him; he re- membered a tree. (Tap finger on side of head.)
He could run and climb it, and then he could see. (Pretend to climb a tree.)

So he did just that, and he sat to wait (cross hands in front of chest),
Hoping to see Jesus before it got too late. (Shade eyes and move head slowly from one side to other.)

When Jesus came by to Zacchaeus, he said ("walk" fingers in front of you),
"Let's go to your house and eat some bread!" (Cup hands to mouth.)

So he went with Jesus, and they ate dinner (march in place),
And he learned that night that he was a sinner. (Put your hands on your chest.)

Zacchaeus decided that very day (clap your hands)
To trust in Jesus and to always obey. (Point up.)

EXTRA IDEA! Create a "sycamore tree" as a prop that children can sit under as you tell the story of Zacchaeus.

From brown poster board, cut out a sycamore tree trunk that is about three feet tall. Use a marker to draw vertical lines of "bark" on the tree trunk. Tape the trunk to the wall. Then cut out or tear leaf shapes and tape them to the top of the tree for leaves. Sit with your children at the foot of the sycamore tree and read the Bible story.

Jesus Knows Us

 Have children sit in a circle. Tell kids the story found in Luke 19:1-10. Afterward, establish a rhythm by having children slap their thighs twice and clap once. Once they're comfortable with the rhythm, introduce this chant:

**Je-sus knew Zacc-hae-us
Je-sus knows** [child's name]**.**

Go around the circle until you've said each child's name.

Affirm a Parent

 Remind your children that Jesus showed he liked Zacchaeus by want- ing to spend time with him and get- ting to know him. Ask your children to think of one or two things that they like about you while you think of things you like about them. Take turns saying, "I like you because…"

Coin Collecting

 Here's a fund-raiser your children will enjoy that reinforces the Bible story of Zacchaeus the tax collector. Designate a safe place where there won't be younger children that might put money in their mouths. Rope off the area. An- nounce to the congregation that your class is raising money to purchase a needed item for the classroom, a missions child, or a local charity. Tell the congregation they are invited to come to [your designated area] after the service where they can scatter their coins for the children to collect (like an egg hunt). At the end of class, tell children that they will collect money for your fund-raiser. Go to the designated area, and let children collect all the coins in small baggies or their craft purses if they made them. Then give the money back the way Zacchaeus did so that the [name of item] can be purchased.

THE EASTER STORY

Matthew 21:1-11; 27:27-56; 28:1-10; Mark 11:1-11; 16:1-8;
Luke 19:28-40; 23:1-49; and John 20:19-31

Passover time was drawing near—
it was less than a week away!
So Jesus and his followers went to Jerusalem to stay.

But before they reached the city gates,
Jesus sent two men ahead.
"You'll find a donkey and colt close by.
Bring them to me," he said.

The disciples found the donkey and a young colt by its side.
They laid their coats on the young colt's back,
then Jesus got on to ride.

As Jesus rode into the city,
the crowd started buzzing and humming.
"Look, it's Jesus!" the people cried.
"Our King is finally coming!"

Some people took off their coats and laid them in the street.
They added leafy palms to the path for the donkey's feet.

The people cried, "Hosanna! Jesus comes in the name of the Lord!"
Everyone cheered and gladly showed it was Jesus they adored.

Later Jesus' friends gathered in an upper room to eat.
Jesus tried to explain that this was the last time they would meet.

As the men enjoyed their dinner, Jesus gave thanks for the bread.
He gave his friends a cup to drink; "Remember me," he said.

"Tonight you'll turn away from me—yes, Peter, you'll go too.
Three times you'll say you don't know me before the night is through."

Then Jesus took his closest friends to a garden where he could pray.
He asked them to watch and to stay awake, and then he walked away.

"It's late," the disciples mumbled. "We can't stay awake—this is boring."
Before they knew it, their eyes were closed, and the three sleepy men were snoring!

Then an angry crowd came to the place where Jesus knelt to pray.
When the disciples saw the soldiers' swords, they turned and ran away.

The angry crowd put Jesus on trial; they wanted him to die.
When Jesus said he was God's Son, they thought it was a lie!

The mob took Jesus to Pilate—the governor of the land.
Pilate said, "This man has done no wrong!"
But the crowd didn't understand.

"Why should we kill this Jesus?" a troubled Pilate cried.
The angry crowd shouted louder and louder, "Let him be crucified!"

The soldiers made a thorny crown
to press on Jesus' head. They hurt
him and they laughed at him.
"Hail, King of the Jews!" they said.

Three days after Jesus died,
some women went to see
The tomb where Jesus' body was.
(Or where they thought that it would be!)

But when the women got to the tomb,
They found it open wide!
The great big stone had been rolled away;
Jesus' body wasn't inside!

Then two shining angels appeared,
And this is what they said:
"You are looking here for Jesus,
But he's risen from the dead!"

Later two men who knew Jesus
Walked down Emmaus road.
Their hearts were sad and lonely;
Their grief was a heavy load.

Another man joined them
And asked, "What are you talking about?"
They answered, "Some say our Lord is alive;
We just can't figure it out!"

Then the stranger explained the Scriptures
So the men could understand,
That Jesus died and rose again
Just as God had planned.

That night they shared dinner together,
And when Jesus broke the bread,
The two men recognized Jesus—
He *had* risen from the dead!

Hosanna to the King

 Bring in a riding toy to represent the donkey. Have your children take turns riding the toy around the outside of the circle each time you repeat the song. Let them sit in a circle clapping their hands to the rhythm as they sing the following song to the tune of "Old MacDonald."

**Here comes Jesus. Hail the King!
Hosanna to the King!
Here comes Jesus. Let's all sing
Hosanna to the King!**

**Here he comes,
God's own Son.
Sing his praises,
Everyone.**

**Here comes Jesus. Let's all sing
Hosanna to the King!**

Jesus Sets Us Free!

 Lead your children in singing this song to the tune of "This Old Man." Encourage them to do the motions with you.

**Jesus died
On the cross** (stretch arms out in cross shape)
To save a world that was lost.
(Make circular motion using both hands.)
He died to show his love for you and me (place hands over heart)
And from sin to set us free! (Hold hands up high over head.)

Jesus Gives New Life

 Lead children in singing the following song to "This Old Man." Lead children in the motions.

Jesus came. (Clap three times.)
Praise his name! (Clap three times.)
I will never be the same. (Shake head from side to side.)
Jesus died to take my sins away.
(Hold arms out to form cross, then pretend to toss something away.)
Jesus gives new life today. (Point to heaven, then cross arms on chest.)

Celebrate! (Wave hands in air.)
Celebrate! (Wave hands in air.)
Thank God for this special date!
(Clap seven times.)
Jesus rose again on Easter day.
(Raise arms with palms up.)
Jesus gives new life today. (Point to heaven, then cross arms on chest.)

EXTRA IDEA! Here's a fun song your children will enjoy singing to the tune of "London Bridge."

**Jesus died and rose again,
Rose again, rose again.
Jesus died and rose again.
I believe it!**

Let's Pray!

Who Needs to Know?

Have children stand in a circle. Ask them to think of people who need to know that Jesus is alive. Tell children that they will toss a large empty plastic egg to each other and say the person's name during the prayer.

**Dear God,
Help us to tell the exciting news that Jesus is alive to all our friends.** Let each child toss the empty egg to one another and say the name of his or her person. Have kids continue tossing the egg until they all have had a chance to say their person's name. **In Jesus' name, amen.**

A Prayer for a King

Punch a hole in the center of a cross for each child. Give each child two twelve-inch chenille wires and a cross. Show the children how to thread the chenille wires through their crosses, and then wrap the ends of the wires together to make one long wire. Help children bend the wires into pointed crowns with the cross in the center. As children finish bending the wires, help them wrap the crowns around their heads. Remind the children that Jesus is our king who died for us. Have kids wear their crowns around their heads as you lead them in saying the following prayer:

Dear God, thank you for Jesus, who gave his life so we can be forgiven for the wrong things we do. We're glad that Jesus is our King who lives in heaven. In Jesus' name, amen.

New Ways to Pray

✔ Have children sit in a circle. Pass a small loaf of bread around, and have each child break off a piece. Let children eat their bread. Tell your children that each time they take a bite of bread they can remember that Jesus wants us to remember him and believe in him. Ask your children to tell God what they remember about Jesus and thank him for loving them.

✔ If you have photos, slides, or home videos of past church events bring a few in to show your children. Encourage your family to remember all the fun times you've had together at church. Talk about why it's important to remember important moments. Thank God for fun church times.

✔ Take your children on a short Easter prayer walk together. Walk around your church or neighborhood, and find a quiet spot to sit and pray. Remind your children of the beautiful garden where Jesus went to pray. Thank God for sending Jesus to die for us and rise again so that we can be forgiven and live in heaven with him.

Let's Play!

Thanks for Serving!

Have your kids make several extra Puzzle-Piece Crosses to give to the teachers who served in the class this Easter. Write on the backs of the crosses, "Thanks for telling us today that Jesus is alive!"

Puzzle–Piece Cross

Ahead of time, cut one cardboard cross for each child, and punch a hole in the top. Have children glue old puzzle pieces to the crosses to fill in the shape. Encourage kids to overlap the puzzle pieces to create more dimension. When the glue has dried, tie yarn through the top of each cross so children can hang the crosses in their bedroom windows when they go home. Remind children that Jesus had to die on the cross for our sin but then he rose again and provided forgiveness and life with him forever.

EXTRA IDEA! Give each child a sheet of construction paper that's not green or purple. Set out glue sticks and scraps of green and purple construction paper. Have children tear grape shapes from the purple paper and leaf shapes from the green paper, and glue the shapes to their construction paper place mats. Help children write their initials on their place mats. As children work, talk about the special meal that Jesus and his disciples shared. If you have time, cut pieces of clear contact paper about an inch larger than the place mats, and laminate them for the children.

Jesus Is Risen!

Have your children form a circle and sit down. Turn on a cassette or CD player to the children's favorite "Jesus songs." While the music plays, have your children pass three or four plastic eggs around the circle. Each time you randomly stop the music, have children open the plastic eggs and shout, "Jesus is alive!" Continue to play until everyone has had a few turns to open an egg.

Empty Tombs

Open a 12-ounce box of vanilla wafers, and set aside 1 cookie for each family member. Then let your child crush the remaining cookies, and mix with ¾ cup grated coconut, ¾ cup powdered sugar, and ½ cup thawed orange juice concentrate.

Have your child roll small lumps of the dough into balls. Then have your child press his or her thumb in the dough to create "empty tombs." Distribute whole vanilla wafers, and let family members cover their empty tombs with vanilla wafer "stones." Encourage family members to uncover their tombs as they tell the Easter story.

Jesus Is Alive!

Call local florists, and ask if they will donate carnations or other single-stemmed flowers to give to your church's congregation. (Or you can purchase the flowers.) After the service, let your class stand inside the church doors and give flowers to families as they leave. Encourage each child to say, "Jesus is alive!" as the person is handed a flower.

How PETER Served JESUS

Acts 3:1-9; 9:36-43; 12:1-18

Every afternoon at 3 o'clock, Peter and John went to the Temple to pray. They always saw a man who couldn't walk sitting by the gate begging money. Peter and John told the lame man they had no money but would give him something much better. What do you think they gave him?

Peter commanded, "By Jesus' power, stand up and walk!" Peter took the man's hand and lifted him up. Right away the man's legs became strong! The man jumped up and scurried all around the Temple courts, walking and jumping and praising God. It was the happiest day of his life—but some people at the Temple weren't happy at all.

The Temple leaders were jealous. All the people in the Temple were amazed to see the beggar walking and jumping. Everyone listened as Peter told about Jesus. The Temple guards arrested Peter and John and kept them in jail for a night. The Temple leaders warned Peter and John to stop talking about Jesus, but they didn't stop. They served Jesus by telling more people about him.

Peter traveled to other towns to tell about Jesus. In one town he heard about a woman named Tabitha who made clothes for poor people. When Tabitha died, her friends begged Peter to help. Peter knelt and prayed beside Tabitha's bed, then commanded her to stand up. And by Jesus' power, Tabitha opened her eyes and came alive! Many people heard what happened and started believing in Jesus.

Wicked King Herod put Peter in jail for serving Jesus. Peter slept in chains between two soldiers, while more soldiers guarded the door. Suddenly a bright light filled Peter's cell. An angel appeared and awakened Peter. The chains fell off his hands. Clankety clank! The angel led Peter past the guards and out of jail. What an exciting escape! Peter went to Mary's house to tell his friends that he was free.

Peter knocked at Mary's door. A servant girl named Rhoda was so happy to hear Peter's voice that she forgot to open the door! Instead, she ran to tell everyone that Peter was there. They opened the door, and Peter hushed the amazed people. He told them that God sent an angel to free him. Peter was able to serve Jesus again!

God Sends His Angels

 Lead your children in singing the following tune to "He's Got the Whole World."

God sends his angels to help us.
God sends his angels to help us.
God sends his angels to help us.
God is watching over us.

We know that God loves us. Yes,
he does!
We know that God loves us. Yes,
he does!
We know that God loves us. Yes,
he does!
God is watching over us.

Will You Get Up?

 Sing this song with your child to the tune of "Mulberry Bush."

Tabitha, will you get up?
Will you get up? Will you get up?
Tabitha, will you get up?
Will you get up today?

We Can Pray

 Tell your children that they will get a chance to say their own prayers to God at the end of the song. Sing the following song to the tune of "When the Saints Go Marching In."

Oh, we can pray
To God all day.
Our God is never far away.
In Taiwan, Peru, or Norway,
God will hear just what we say.

Oh, we can pray
To God all day.
Our God is never far away.
There's no need for us to delay.
Who will pray right now, today?

(Let kids take turns saying spontaneous prayers.)

Let's Pray!

God Is With Me

Gather children together in a circle. Have them repeat each line of the prayer after you.

**Thank you, God,
For being with me.
You helped Peter
And gave him bravery.
And if I ask,
You'll help me, too.
There is nothing
I can't do.
Thank you, God!
Amen.**

A Lame Man's Prayer

Have your children sit in a circle. Let each of the children take turns lying on a mat or a beach towel you've brought from home. While children take their turn on the mat, encourage them to thank Jesus for giving them legs to walk and a family to take care of them. At the end of each child's prayer, choose a child to help the "lame" child up as Peter helped the lame man up.

New Ways to Pray

✔ Distribute crepe paper streamers to family members. Have each person take turns waving the ribbons in the air and praying, "Thank you, God, for hearing my prayers."

✔ Pass an angel figure around the circle, and lead the children in thanking God for sending his angel to help us.

✔ Let kids take turns praying for people they know are sick. Pass a stethoscope around the circle and let the child on the right side of the praying child place the stethoscope on the praying child's back and listen as he or she prays. Continue passing the stethoscope around the circle until all the children have had a chance to pray and listen with the stethoscope.

Let's Play!

Peter Is Free!

Give your child a sheet of sandpaper and five pieces of yarn, each piece about ten inches long. Set out crayons to share. Begin telling the Bible story of Peter being put in prison. Pause and have your child draw a picture of Peter on the sandpaper. When he or she has drawn Peter, continue the story. Have your child place the pieces of yarn over the drawing to show when Peter was put in jail. When the angel takes Peter out of jail, direct your child to remove the yarn bars from the "jail."

Peter, Peter, Angel

 Have your children sit in a circle. Choose a "Tapper" to walk around the outside of the circle, tapping the children's heads and saying "Peter." When the Tapper taps someone and says "Angel," the Angel should get up, put an arm around the Tapper, and walk around the circle once with the Tapper. Then the Angel becomes the Tapper. Continue until all the children have been Tappers and Angels.

Pop Up, Tabitha

 Have your child draw a face on one index finger with a fine-tip marker. Demonstrate how to start the finger play by closing the fist to hide the drawn face. Then lead your child in doing the following motions.

Pop up, Tabitha! God heard Peter's prayer. *(Lift only index finger.)*
Don't hide under the covers!
  Please come out of there. *(Hide index finger in fist.)*
Dance a little dance! *(Bring out index finger and wiggle it in your fist.)*
Turn around and around! *(Turn hand.)*
God has healed your body,
So make a happy sound. *(Clap and cheer!)*

Tabitha Snacks

 Prepare two baking pans of gelatin using the "Jell-O Jigglers" snack recipe. Use a girl-shaped cookie cutter and a spatula.

Have your child wash his or her hands (or use wet wipes). Have family members gather around the pans of gelatin and, one at a time, press the cookie cutter into the gelatin. Let each person lift a "Tabitha" from the pan and place it on a small paper plate. Each time a Tabitha is lifted, remind everyone that God raised Tabitha from the dead.

I'll Pray for You

 Help your children learn that they can pray for each other anytime, for any reason. Remind kids that Peter prayed for the lame man and Tabitha and that Peter's friends prayed for him. Set out crayons, safety scissors, and 8½x11 sheets of colored paper. Demonstrate how to fold the paper in half horizontally and place a hand down on the fold with closed fingers to make "praying hands." Encourage your children to work with partners if they need help tracing their hands. Help your children cut out their praying hands, being careful not to cut off the fold. Ask each child to choose one person in your church to pray for this week and draw the person's picture inside the praying hands. Have your children pray for the people they picked. Encourage them to give their praying hands to the people and tell them that they prayed for them.

Tell-It Treats

 Have family members make "Tell-It Treats" to share with their neighbors. Create paper heart-shapes with the words "Jesus loves you" on them. Give each person a sturdy plate and graham crackers. Ask them to decorate the graham crackers with canned frosting and colorful sprinkles or raisins. Place plastic wrap around the plates. Help younger children write their names or initials on the heart-shapes and tape the hearts on the plastic. Then take the snack plates to your neighbors.